AMERICA THE BEAUTIFUL

In the words of

JOHN F. KENNEDY

By the Editors of COUNTRY BEAUTIFUL Magazine
Editorial Direction: Michael P. Dineen
Edited by Robert L. Polley
Art Direction and Design by Robert N. Taylor

Published by Country Beautiful Foundation, Inc., Elm Grove, Wisconsin

COUNTRY BEAUTIFUL
MAGAZINE

President: Arthur J. Schmid Jr.

Publisher & Editorial Director: Michael P. Dineen

Executive Editor: Robert L. Polley

Art Director: Robert N. Taylor

Managing Editor: Dana F. Kellerman

Senior Editors: Kenneth L. Schmitz   James H. Robb,

Associate Editors: Virginia Downing, Lawrence A. Westbrook

Editorial Assistant: Sandra L. Collins *Copy reader:* Joanne Schweik

Staff: Sharon L. Griswold, Marilyn Hyland, Kristin Rasmussen, Lovelace White

COUNTRY BEAUTIFUL Magazine is published by Country Beautiful Foundation, Inc., 15330 Watertown Plank Rd., Elm Grove, Wis., a nonprofit organization dedicated to strengthening and preserving the physical, cultural and moral values of America and other nations of the world. COUNTRY BEAUTIFUL FOUNDATION, INC. Officers and Directors: Charles H. Kellstadt, Carl N. Jacobs, Arthur J. Schmid Jr., Edward C. Ramacher, Michael P. Dineen, Cy Crawford, Wilfred A. Schuster.

Grateful acknowledgment is made to the following, without whom this book would not be possible: Stewart L. Udall, Secretary of the Interior; James K. Carr, Under Secretary of the Interior; Richard Cardinal Cushing; John M. Kauffmann, National Park Service; William M. Donnelly, Assistant Information Officer, Office of Saline Water; James N. Faber, Assistant to the Secretary and Director of Information, U.S. Department of the Interior; Russell T. Forte, Picture Editor, Photography Division, U.S. Department of Agriculture; Mrs. Harold P. Ganss, White House Press Office; John T. Houbolt, Chief, Branch of Still and Motion Pictures, National Park Service; Wilbur P. Kane, Assistant Commissioner, Bureau of Reclamation; O. B. Lloyd Jr., Director, Public Information, NASA Headquarters; Ray Mackland, Director, Press and Publications, U.S. Information Agency; Charles T. Myers Jr., Chief, Photography Division, U.S. Department of Agriculture; Mrs. Carol J. Smith, Acting Chief, Division of Information and Publications, National Capital Region, National Park Service; Carlos Whiting, Chief of Press Relations, National Park Service.

The Editors would like to thank the following publishers for permission to quote from their publications: Anti-Defamation League of B'nai B'rith for excerpts from *A Nation of Immigrants* published in 1959, reprinted from *A Nation of Immigrants* by permission of the Anti-Defamation League of B'nai B'rith. Cowles Magazines and Broadcasting Inc. for excerpt from "Physical Fitness: A Report of Progress," published in Look Magazine, August 13, 1963, copyright, 1963, by Cowles Magazines and Broadcasting Inc. Foreign Service Journal for excerpt from an address given by President Kennedy to the American Foreign Service Association on May 31, 1962. Holt, Rinehart and Winston, Inc. for excerpts from *The Quiet Crisis* by Stewart L. Udall, published in 1963 and for excerpt from the poem, "Sand Dunes" from *Complete Poems of Robert Frost.* Copyright 1928 by Holt, Rinehart and Winston, Inc. Copyright renewed© 1956 by Robert Frost. Reprinted by permission of Holt, Rinehart and Winston, Inc. Parade Publications, Inc. for excerpts from "John F. Kennedy Tells Youth How to Prepare for the Presidency," published in Parade Magazine September 23, 1962. The Ridge Press, Inc. for excerpts from *Creative America,* published in 1963. Saturday Review for excerpt from book review, published September 3, 1960, of *Deterrent or Defense* by B. H. Liddell Hart.

We dedicate this book to Jacqueline Kennedy, not so much in praise of her limitless courage at the time of her husband's death but more in payment for a real and very personal debt. She was the one who might have been most bitter, most broken, but she showed us how to accept; she went on, and her courage helped our nation continue. Jacqueline Kennedy did not speak. Yet her eloquent black figure and her face under the veil told us what we needed to know: that we must face this, and pray, and trust in God, and go forward. This book is dedicated to Jacqueline Kennedy, in gratitude.

A family for the ages—proud, young and full of life

Mr. Kennedy and daughter surrounded
by neighbors outside of the Cape Cod
home of his father, Joseph P. Kennedy.

The First Family after attending church in Florida in April 1963.

Eighteen-month-old "John-John"
during his first visit to the
President's White House office.

White House Photo: Abbie Rowe

On October 17, 1963 Mrs. Kennedy is greeted at Washington, D.C., airport by her family on her return from Greece.

Wide World

Mrs. Kennedy and Caroline in New York in 1962 prior to their vacation in Italy.

Wide World

Ted Polumbaum-Pix

The President and Mrs. Kennedy relax in the yard with their daughter, Caroline, and her two kittens.

President and daughter visit Mrs. Kennedy at Otis Air Force Base hospital.

CONTENTS

JOHN F. KENNEDY: In Memoriam

John Fitzgerald Kennedy's legacy to the brotherhood of man will unfold, as Lincoln's did, with the passing of time. The ennobling influence of his vibrant life and tragic death has reached around the world already.

Our youngest elected President had but three short years in office. But in that time he presented to the world an indelible picture of America as a youthful, vital and steadfast nation.

His idealism inspired us all in the struggle for a better world and a more just society.

He enhanced respect, in ourselves and in each other, for individual excellence, and he heightened our determination to elevate the quality of American life.

His unrelenting search for the wellsprings of wisdom accentuated our interest in philosophers, poets and statesmen.

A man of peace, he knew that world order was possible only if strong nations respected the weak and exercised power both with courage and restraint. He taught us that the family of nations must understand each other's institutions, history and national differences.

He dedicated himself to the public service, and inspired his fellow men to put the good of the community first.

By the example of his life John F. Kennedy still lives in our quest for justice and equality and excellence and brotherhood.

Sincerely

Lyndon B. Johnson

LYNDON B. JOHNSON
THE WHITE HOUSE
January 1964

INTRODUCTION

JOHN F. KENNEDY

AND AMERICA THE BEAUTIFUL

The New Frontier of John Fitzgerald Kennedy encompassed such complex problems as automation, outer space and nuclear testing—and was dominated by the overriding quest for peace through the use of power and diplomacy. Yet, engrossed as he became in the struggle for world order, President Kennedy found time to involve himself deeply in the land and people problems of his own country.

Our Presidents have differed in their concern over our inherited resources. Some have left a record of mismanagement, waste and giveaway; others have sought to teach their fellow men better practices of husbandry and higher concepts of conservation.

If John Kennedy had a particular attachment to his continent it was to its seashores and the marginal sea. He grew to manhood on the Atlantic Coast, and mastered a seaman's skills in time of war. When he sought solitude or a renewal of the spirit, more often than not he found it amid the fresh winds and dependable tides of the seashore.

As a Senator he sought to insure that his countrymen would have an everlasting opportunity to share the outdoor experience he prized most when he championed the fight to establish a Cape Cod National Seashore. One of the supreme satisfactions of his Presidency came when he signed the Cape Cod bill into law one summer day in 1961.

The Cape Cod Seashore signified more for President Kennedy than the preservation of a superb scenic area that he knew and loved. He saw it as a triumph for the millions of urban Americans whose access to the out of doors was being curtailed.

This experience convinced him of the national need to establish other Cape Cods in all parts of our land. He recognized that America would be an urban-centered nation of 300 million people in 30 years. He had the foresight to realize that our conservation policies had to ensure that our city-bound citizens would have an over-all environment that would enrich and enliven their lives.

During his Administration he proposed the pioneering open space program, which was a first step toward a balanced urban environment. He also gave strong support to the battle against air and water pollution, and he launched a program to alleviate city congestion through efficient mass transit.

President Kennedy also realized that science had to become the hand-maiden of conservation in his time. Scientific research was uncovering new sources of energy and new uses for resources. The desalination of sea water, the extraction of oil from shale rock, the positive uses of atomic energy—these were techniques which he believed were opening up a new era of resource management.

In conservation, as in his general outlook on American life, John Kennedy looked to the future with optimism. He deeply believed that it was possible for the American people to build the foundations of a truly great civilization.

A few weeks before his death President Kennedy summed up his aspiration for the nation he governed:

> "*I look forward*," he said, "*to a great future for America, a future in which our country will match its military strength with our moral strength, its wealth with our wisdom, its power with our purpose. I look forward to an America which will not be afraid of grace and beauty, which will protect the beauty of our natural environment, which will preserve the great old American houses and squares and parks of our national past, and which will build handsome and balanced cities for our future. . . . And I look forward to an America which commands respect throughout the world not only for its strength but for its civilization as well.*"

Is it too much to hope that the American people will take up this challenge, and help turn this vision of our martyred President into a reality?

STEWART L. UDALL
WASHINGTON, D.C.
January 1964

Our
Commitment
to Future
Generations

By JOHN F. KENNEDY

Robert Frost, the late poet, once remarked, "What makes a nation in the beginning is a good piece of geography." Americans have been richly endowed with a land that is both beauteous and bountiful. Our greatness today rests in part on this gift of geography that is the United States; but what is important for tomorrow is what the people of America do with their conservation legacy.

At the turn of the century, Theodore Roosevelt and Gifford Pinchot halted the waste of some resources, and established national conservation programs in forestry and wildlife that were a solid success. A generation later, the alphabetical agencies of Franklin D. Roosevelt rebuilt damaged parts of our land, and huge dams and development projects were begun that are now the sinews of our national economy. There were wise conservationists, but it was Pinchot, in those early 1900s, who also emphasized that the cause of conservation would

United States Department of the Interior, National Park Service Photo

ultimately fail unless every generation of Americans made a conservation commitment to the future. In his time, Franklin Roosevelt was making such a commitment, and now in the 1960s, I hope that we too will make comparably wise decisions for the future of our country.

We live in a period of global danger. Our policies in this context are quite simple. Our objective abroad is to protect the security and vital interests of the United States, and to maintain the peace. We do that by increasing the posture of the United States through military build-ups and alliances and commitments to friends overseas. Behind this shield, all the improvements in our defensive strength, all our guarantees, all our alliances, are of no use unless the United States itself is a prosperous, virile and growing society. To be sure of that requires attention to our problems here at home.

Our national population today is 190 million. In the time of Franklin Roosevelt it was 130 million. By the year 2000 it will be 350 million people, living where 190 million lived, or 130 million, or where only 80 million lived 60 or 70 years ago. This tremendous increment is devouring the resources of our country, including precious living space itself.

National growth and the fantastic surge of science have now made conservation problems and opportunities infinitely complex—and enormously challenging. The task of propelling a third wave of the conservation movement in the 1960s is to make science the servant of conservation and to devise new programs of land stewardship that will enable us to preserve an environment that will renew and inspire the human enterprise.

After concentrating on conservation problems, after viewing places of scenic wonder and the wonders of modern science, it seems to me that three major conclusions can be drawn:

First, we must mount a new campaign to preserve a natural environment worthy of the wealthiest nation on earth.

Second, we must recognize that the best way to quicken the conservation of resources is to hasten the conservation of man through wise programs of education that will develop the finest and highest talents of all of our people.

Third, we must seize suitable opportunities to advance world order by encouraging international cooperation in programs of resource conservation.

On every hand we see forces at work that tend to despoil and pollute and blight parts of our land. As good stewards of our land heritage, we must take aggressive action to set aside the prime park, seashore, wildlife, forest and outdoor recreation lands which present and future generations will need. Our irreplaceable wilderness lands need permanent status protection, and a Youth Conservation Corps should be established to rehabilitate and renew our public estate. Conservation must be applied in our city environments in a concerted fight against urban forms of pollution and disorder and decay.

Today our very capacity to "create" new resources and to help technology hand us the keys to the kingdom of abundance rests on the success of our system of education. Human resources and natural resources are inexorably intertwined, and tomorrow's children, if they are to manage this land well, will need the precision of scientifically attuned minds, coupled with a sensitivity to their fellow man and creatures. We have started the construction of the world's largest nuclear power plant, and the continuing revolution in research will soon enable us to harness the tides at Passamaquoddy,* interconnect the electric power systems of whole regions, extract low cost fresh water from the seas, turn vast oil shale beds into oil and "breed" energy from stones. Human talents are enhancing the use of our resources to meet the complex requirements of the future.

In the years ahead our achievements will depend more and more on the success of peoples throughout the world in dealing with their resources. We are already sharing our surpluses and our science with friendly nations, and the Peace Corps program and the current phase of our foreign aid effort largely involve the export of conservation techniques. Technology and science are compelling us to do international conservation planning: The Treaty that made the Antarctic a scientific preserve, and the International Geophysical Year program have helped inspire world order; and the Test Ban Treaty was also a triumph for conservation, for, hopefully, it will reduce radioactive pollution of the one resource that all mankind shares—the atmosphere itself.

If we have the vision and the energy to implement such a new wave of conservation effort, in our time we can make America a more green and pleasant and productive land.

*A bay on the coast of Maine.

...ctary of the Interior James K. Carr (center) guides Mr. Kennedy and ...her dignitaries during the President's 1963 conservation tour.

...ican people are not by nature wasteful . . .

...gement Photo: Jim Lee

Government must provide a national policy framework for this new conservation emphasis; but in the final analysis, it must be done by the people themselves. The American people are not by nature wasteful. They are not unappreciative of our inheritance, but unless we, as a country, with the support and sometimes the direction of Government, [work] with state leaders, [work] with the community, [work] with all our citizens, we are going to leave an entirely different inheritance in the next 25 years than the one we found.

Pinchot Institute for Conservation Studies,
Milford, Pennsylvania, Sept. 24, 1963

It is not always the other person who pollutes our streams, or litters our highways, or throws away a match in a forest, or wipes out game, or wipes out our fishing reserves.

Pinchot Institute for Conservation Studies,
Milford, Pennsylvania, Sept. 24, 1963

All these subjects do not have the drama of the great struggle over the Nuclear Test Ban Treaty, but these are the hard jobs of government, and this country will be able to fulfill its responsibilities as a great, free society if we take care of the matters back home. And if we take care of the undramatic matters which make the difference between life and death in a community and happiness or depression for a family.

Northern Great Lakes Region Land and People Conference,
University of Minnesota, Duluth, Minnesota, Sept. 24, 1963

Secretary Udall,
...tter has reached such
...other generation
...f junk will be
...y of any person
...the

The National Park System preserves the remains of previous cultures, such as these Pueblo cliff dwellings in Mesa Verde National Park in Colorado.

I

Man and the Land

"Our greatness today rests in part on this gift of geography that is the United States...."

From "Our Commitment to Future Generations"

In an appearance before a farm group John F. Kennedy, while a Senator, humorously described himself as "a city boy from an Eastern state who has never milked a cow or plowed a furrow, straight or crooked." But no President since Theodore Roosevelt had as much concern for the land, in the largest sense of that word. His own personal experience with the sea and the lands that touch the sea yielded joy and challenge and helped to give him values that contributed immeasurably to all aspects of his public and private life. These same values helped him to be vividly aware of the daily tragedy of hunger in those countries which lack the abundance provided by the American earth and to recognize the need for vigilance and foresight in the preservation of our natural resources.

From the beginning, Americans
had a lively awareness of the land . . .

The earth can be an abundant mother . . . if we learn to use her with skill and wisdom, to heal her wounds, replenish her vitality and utilize her potentialities. . . . This seems to me the greatest challenge . . . to use the world's resources, to expand life and hope for the world's inhabitants.

National Academy of Sciences, Washington, D.C., Oct. 22, 1963

The history of America is, more than that of most nations, the history of man confronted by nature. . . .

From the beginning, Americans had a lively awareness of the land and the wilderness. The Jeffersonian faith in the independent farmer laid the foundation for American democracy; and the ever-beckoning, ever-receding frontier left an indelible imprint on American society and the American character. And Americans pioneered in more than the usual way. We hear much about "land reform" today in other parts of the world; but we do not perhaps reflect enough on the extent to which land reform, from the Northwest Ordinance through the Homestead Act of the Farm Security Administration and beyond, was an American custom and an American innovation.

Introduction to a book, The Quiet Crisis, by Stewart L. Udall,
Holt, Rinehart and Winston, 1963

Our growth, private enterprise system, the governmental relationship to it, particularly the governmental relationship which has developed over the last 50 years, represents a very special blend of our population, our skills, our natural resources.

Association for International Exchange of Students in
Economics and Commerce, Washington, D.C., April 10, 1963

Marshal Lyautey, who was the great French Marshal in North Africa, was once talking to his gardener and he suggested that he plant a tree, and the gardener said, "Well, why plant it? It won't flower for 100 years." And Marshal Lyautey said, "In that case, plant it this afternoon."

University of North Dakota, Grand Forks,
North Dakota, Sept. 25, 1963

Projects by the Bureau of Reclamation, such as the Arrowrock Dam in Idaho, insure that there is enough clean water to serve the human and industrial needs of an area.

Under Sec
o

The Amer

Bureau of Land Man

According to Interior
". . . Our landscape i
proportions that in an
a trash pile or piece o
within a stone's thro
standing anywhere o
American land mass.

20

This continent is a Nation of nations which you must see and know . . .

The great movements in this country's history, the great periods of intellectual and social activity, took place in those periods when we looked long range to the future. . . . It was in the days of Theodore Roosevelt, when the whole national conservation movement began, and all of the decisions [were made] in a much easier period, when we had far fewer people . . . which makes it possible for us to travel throughout the United States and still see green grass and still have some hope for the future.

I want us in 1963 to make the same decisions here in the United States for the use of our manpower, for the use of our natural resources, for the strengthening of the United States, so that the United States can bear the burdens which go with being the most powerful country in the free world. . . .

Tacoma, Washington, Sept. 27, 1963

Theodore Roosevelt, one of the great conservationist Presidents, in Yosemite National Park in California.

I have come on a journey of five days across the United States, beginning in Pennsylvania and ending in California, to talk about the conservation of our resources, and I think it is appropriate that we should come here to North Dakota where this whole struggle for the maintenance of the natural resources of this country, for the development of the natural resources of this country, in a sense, began. I do not argue whether it was Harvard University or North Dakota that made Theodore Roosevelt such a man and such a conservationist, but I am sure that his years here in North Dakota helped make him realize how expensive, how wasteful was indifference to this great resource and how valuable it could become. He put it on much more than a material plane. He said it was the moral obligation of a society in order to preserve that society to maintain its natural endowment.

University of North Dakota, Grand Forks,
North Dakota, Sept. 25, 1963

It was one of the great strengths of a President such as Theodore Roosevelt that he knew and loved the diverse magnificence of our fields and mountain ranges, deserts and great rivers, our abundant farmlands and the thousand voices of our cities. No revolution in communication or transportation can destroy the fact that this continent is, as Whitman said, "a Nation of nations," which you must see and know before you can govern.

"John F. Kennedy Tells Youth How to Prepare for the Presidency,"
an article in Parade Magazine, Sept. 23, 1962

The lands conserved as national parks are developed, wherever appropriate, for recreational use, for as Under Secretary of the Interior James K. Carr has said, "When we talk about conservation, we mean development of resources as well as preservation."

Antipollution programs are
necessary to insure clean streams
and lakes for fishing and recreation.

A stand of sequoia trees, which
are among the largest and oldest
living things, is ideal for a nature walk.

We are reaching the limits
of our fundamental needs . . .

There are two points on conservation that have come home
to me in the last two days. One is the necessity for us to protect what
we already have, what nature gave to us, and use it well, not to
waste water or land, to set aside land and water, recreation, wilderness and all the rest now so that it will be available to those who
come in the future. That is the traditional concept of conservation,
and it still has a major part in the national life of the United States.
But the other part of conservation is the newer part, and that is to use
science and technology to achieve significant breakthroughs as we
are doing today and in that way to conserve the resources which 10
or 20 or 30 years ago may have been wholly unknown. So we use
nuclear power for peaceful purposes and power. We use techniques to
develop new kinds of coal and oil from shale, and all the rest. We use
new techniques that Senator Magnuson has pioneered in oceanog-
raphy so from the bottom of the ocean and the ocean we get all the
resources which are there, and which are going to be mined and
harvested. And from the sun we are going to find more and more
uses for that energy whose power we are so conscious of today.

Hanford, Washington, Sept. 26, 1963

Our primary task now is to increase our understanding of
our environment, to a point where we can enjoy it without defacing
it, use its bounty without detracting permanently from its value, and,
above all, maintain a living balance between man's actions and
nature's reactions, for this nation's great resource is as elastic and
productive as our ingenuity can make it.

University of Wyoming, Laramie, Wyoming, Sept. 25, 1963

. . . We are reaching the limits of our fundamental needs—of
water to drink, of fresh air to breathe, of open space to enjoy, of
abundant sources of energy to make life easier.

Pinchot Institute for Conservation Studies,
Milford, Pennsylvania, Sept. 24, 1963

Recreational facilities near to urban areas can provide a welcome retreat for the entire family.

National Park Service Photos

Many birds and animals, including bears, elk and buffaloes, have survived the onslaught of civilization primarily because of the many national parks which serve as wildlife sanctuaries.

Our effort must include our complete spectrum of resources . . .

Today's resource problems are closely interrelated. Conservation of our water supplies affects the irrigation of our land and our stocks of fish. Forest development influences power development, and our power development can only be carried out with a careful eye to the need for flood protection and needs of navigation. Soil conservation affects water supply and game supplies for our hunters, as well as our continued ability to meet our food and fiber needs. It is becoming increasingly essential that we consider all our resources in the light of their relationship to each other, as well as to the needs of the economy as a whole and the people as a whole.

Washington, D.C., Oct. 27, 1960

Our national conservation effort must include the complete spectrum of resources: air, water and land; fuels, energy and minerals; soils, forests and forage; fish and wildlife. Together they make up the world of nature which surrounds us—a vital part of the American heritage.

Message to Congress, Washington, D.C., March 1, 1962

If promptly developed, recreational activities and new national park, forest and recreation areas can bolster your economy and provide pleasure for millions of people in the days to come. If we do what is right now, in 1963, we must set aside substantial areas of our country for all the people who are going to live in it by the year 2000. Where 180 million Americans now live, by the year 2000 there will be 350 million of them, and we have to provide for them, as Theodore Roosevelt and Franklin Roosevelt and the others provided for us.

Ashland, Wisconsin, Sept. 24, 1963

"Our forest lands present the sharpest challenge to our foresight," President Kennedy said, because reforestation requires a projection of 40 years into the future before trees, such as these planted along the Ohio River, will be ready for use as timber.

27

To a surprising extent the sea has remained a mystery . . .

Only two per cent of our extraordinary coastline, the Atlantic, the Gulf Stream, and the Pacific, only two per cent is devoted to public use. We have the same fight along our coastlines that we had here in this section of the Northwest 30 and 40 years ago for forests and parks and all the rest. . . .

Great Falls, Montana, Sept. 26, 1963

To a surprising extent, the sea has remained a mystery. Ten thousand fleets still sweep over it in vain. We know less of the oceans at our feet . . . than . . . of the sky above our heads. It is time to change this. . . . A storm along Cape Cod may well begin off the shores of Japan. The world ocean is also indivisible. . . . International scientific cooperation is indispensable if human knowledge of the ocean is to keep pace with human needs.

National Academy of Sciences, Washington, D.C., Oct. 22, 1963

One of the great resources which we are going to find in the next 40 years is not going to be the land; it will be the ocean. We are going to find untold wealth in the oceans of the world which will be used to make a better life for our people. Science is changing all of our natural environment. It can change it for good; it can change it for bad.

University of Wyoming, Laramie, Wyoming, Sept. 25, 1963

Our nation's progress is reflected in the history of our great river systems. The water that courses through our rivers and streams holds the key to full national development. Uncontrolled, it wipes out homes, lives and dreams, bringing disaster in the form of floods; controlled, it is an effective artery of transportation, a boon to industrial development, a source of beauty and recreation and the means for turning arid areas into rich and versatile cropland. In no resource field are conservation principles more applicable. By 1980, it is estimated, our national water needs will nearly double—by the end of the century they will triple. But the quantity of water which nature supplies will remain almost constant.

Message to Congress, Washington, D.C., March 1, 1962

28

Larry Fried—Pix

Point Reyes National Seashore, California.

Jack E. Cole

"Sea waves are green and wet,/But up from where they die,/Rise others vaster yet,/And those are brown and dry." These sand dunes, the late poet Robert Frost said, are "the sea made land."

Cape Cod National Seashore, Massachusetts.

Fort Clatsop National Memorial, Oregon.

The U. S. Soil Conservation Service estimates that erosion damage, as shown in the Texas Blacklands, amounts to $750 million annually.

United States Department of Agriculture Photo: W. E. Jenkins

Our goal: sufficient water in the right place at the right time . . .

Bureau of Reclamation Photo

Irrigation water, so vital to the cultivation of wheat in many areas, is provided by a canal on this Sidney, Montana, farm.

. . . The control of water is the secret of the development of the West, and whether we use it for power or for irrigation or for whatever purpose, no drop of water west of the 100th parallel should flow to the ocean without being used, and to do that requires the dedicated commitment of the people. . . .

Salt Lake City, Utah, Sept. 26, 1963

. . . In the United States, some areas are desperately short of water—and at the same time other areas are ravaged by floods. And our forests are vanishing, our wildlife is vanishing, our streams are polluted and so is the very air we breathe.

Yet America is rich in natural resources. Our impending resource crisis is not due to scarcity. It is due to underdevelopment, despoilment and neglect.

Redding, California, Sept. 8, 1960

Our goal, therefore, is to have sufficient water sufficiently clean in the right place at the right time to serve the range of human and industrial needs. And we must harmonize conflicting objectives— for example, irrigation vs. navigation, multiple-purpose reservoirs vs. scenic park sites. Comprehensive and integrated planning is the only solution of this problem, requiring cooperative efforts at all levels of government.

Message to Congress, Washington, D.C., March 1, 1962

Irrigation projects, such as this one in Yuma Valley, Arizona, have made it possible to raise crops on what formerly was desert.

A strong America depends on its cities—America's glory, and sometimes America's shame. To substitute sunlight for congestion and progress for decay, we have stepped up existing urban renewal and housing programs, and launched new ones. . . .

State of the Union Address to Congress, Washington, D.C., Jan. 11, 1962

The present and future problems of our cities are as complex as they are manifold. There must be expansion: but orderly and planned expansion, not explosion and sprawl. Basic public facilities must be extended ever further into the areas surrounding urban centers: but they must be planned and coordinated so as to favor rather than hamper the sound growth of our communities. The scourge of blight must be overcome, and the central core areas of our cities, with all their great richness of economic and cultural wealth, must be restored to lasting vitality. New values must be created to provide a more efficient local economy and provide revenues to support essential local services. Sound old housing must be conserved and improved, and new housing created, to serve better all income groups in our population and to move ever closer to the goal of a decent home in a suitable living environment for every American family. We will neglect our cities at our peril, for in neglecting them we neglect the nation.

Message to Congress, Washington, D.C., Jan. 30, 1962

In neglecting our cities we neglect the nation . . .

Hundreds of smaller cities and towns are located on or near the fringes of rapidly growing urban areas. The problems of the cities affect them today, and will be theirs tomorrow. Hundreds of other smaller towns and cities not now affected will be so situated a few short years hence.

Message to Congress, Washington, D.C., Jan. 30, 1962

National Park Service Photo: W. E. Dilley

This trip that I have taken is now about 24 hours old, but it is a rewarding 24 hours because there is nothing more encouraging than for . . . us to leave the rather artificial city of Washington and come and travel across the United States and realize what is here, the beauty, the diversity, the wealth, and the vigor of the people. Last Friday I spoke to delegates from all over the world at the United Nations. It is an unfortunate fact that nearly every delegate comes to the United States from all around the world and they make a judgment on the United States based upon an experience in New York or Washington . . . .

University of Wyoming, Laramie, Wyoming, Sept. 25, 1963

President Kennedy visits Grand Teton National Park in Wyoming during his 1963 conservation tour.

The silhouette of a house, torn down during the Independence Mall project in Philadelphia, remains on the wall of an adjoining building.

United States Department of the Interior

Too many people east of the Mississippi

President Kennedy, as he dedicates Whiskeytown Dam and Reservoir, near Redding, California.

We had a 58-hour week, a 48-hour week, a 40-hour week. As machines take more and more of the jobs of men, we are going to find the work week reduced, and we are going to find people wondering what they should do. I want to make it possible . . . for them to see green grass, to travel throughout this great, rich country of ours, not just in other parts of the world, but here in the United States, where I have seen parts of this country which are second to none, to any in the world. . . . Too many people east of the Mississippi are unaware of what golden resources we have in our own United States.

Dedication of Whiskeytown Dam and Reservoir,
Whiskeytown, California, Sept. 28, 1963

. . . In the field of conservation, every day that is lost is a valuable opportunity wasted. Every time, particularly in the East, where they have such concentration of population—every time an acre of land disappears into private development or exploitation, an acre of land which could be used for the people, we have lost a chance. We will never get it back. . . . Land will rise in value, and unless we set it aside and use it wisely today, in 1970 or 1975 we won't have the chance. As you know, along the Atlantic Coast, nearly all of the sea, the beach, is owned by comparatively few people. We were able to set aside, a year ago, Cape Cod Park, which is near to all of the people of New England. We are talking about doing the same now on the Delaware River. We are talking about doing the same in northern Indiana, near Gary. . . . We are talking about now doing the same in northern Wisconsin. . . . We have to seize these opportunities to set aside these wilderness areas, these primitive areas, these fresh water areas, these lakes. We have to set them aside for the people who are going to come after us.

And we have to not only set them aside, but we have to develop them.

University of North Dakota, Grand Forks,
North Dakota, Sept. 25, 1963

34

are unaware of the golden resources in our own United States . . .

One of the most popular national parks, Yosemite in California, is an area of spectacular beauty and grandeur.

Lake Superior, the Apostle Islands, the Bad River area, are all unique. They are worth improving for the benefit of sportsmen and tourists. In an area of congestion and pollution, men make noise and dirt. Lake Superior has a beauty that millions can enjoy. These islands are part of our American heritage. In a very real sense they tell the story of the development of this country. The vast marshes of the Bad River are a rich resource providing a home for a tremendous number and varied number of wild animals. In fact, the entire northern Great Lakes area, with its vast inland sea, its 27,000 lakes and thousands of streams, is a central and significant part of the fresh water assets of this country, and we must act to preserve these assets.

Ashland, Wisconsin, Sept. 24, 1963

I think sometimes we read too much about the problems of particular areas, and maybe North Dakota may not be so interested in the beaches along the Atlantic Coast or along the Gulf, or along the West Coast, and people in the East not so much interested in the Garrison project in North Dakota, which is far away, but this country is not far away. It is closer than it has ever been before. When you can fly across it in five hours, when more important than transportation is the fact that we are one people, living in 50 states and living in hundreds of communities, what happens on the East Coast where your children may someday live, what happens in the Middle West where the children of people in New England may someday live, and what happens on the West Coast are of concern to all of us.

University of North Dakota, Grand Forks,
North Dakota, Sept. 25, 1963

Just as our investment of scientific talent, money and time is better utilized in well-coordinated and complementary programs within the Federal Government and by the closest working relationships with state and local governments, the academic community and industry, so our efforts should be meshed with those of the other countries of the world. Resource conservation problems are worldwide; efforts to solve them should be equally universal. This nation will continue to cooperate in international scientific and research undertakings; and the useful information and specific technological applications we develop—economically feasible desalinization of sea water, for example—will be made available immediately, as has always been our practice, to advance the welfare of all peoples of the world.

Message to Congress, Washington, D.C., March 1, 1962

36

National Park Service Photo: Jack E. Boucher

Desalination of water, as in this Roswell, New Mexico, plant, will open undreamed-of potentialities for man.

Ken Cobean

The rugged beaches and the offshore islands are typical of Olympic National Park in Washington.

*Sometimes we read too much
about the problems of particular areas . . .*

The cause of all mankind
is the cause of America . . .

Any proposed resource development project must, of course, meet the national interest test. It must strengthen the economy of the whole nation and enable America to better compete in the market places of the world.

Washington, D.C., July 16, 1963

. . . I would suggest . . . a worldwide program to protect land and water, forests and wildlife; to combat exhaustion and erosion; to stop the contamination of water and air by industrial as well as nuclear pollution; and to provide for the steady renewal and expansion of the natural bases of life. Malthus argued a century and a half ago that man, by using up all of his available resources, would forever press on the limits of subsistence, thus condemning humanity to an indefinite future of misery and poverty. We can now begin to hope and, I believe, know that Malthus was expressing not a law of nature, but merely the limitation then of scientific and social wisdom.

National Academy of Sciences, Washington, D.C., Oct. 22, 1963

You cannot farm this valley without realizing that there are problems in this valley which can be solved by the united action of all our people, in developing the natural resources. . . . It isn't enough to concern ourselves with what happens in this valley. The United States must also be concerned with what happens in Colombia and the Congo and Indonesia.

One hundred years ago, when this state was founded, the people who came here worried about their farms. Now we have to concern ourselves with the whole globe around us. . . . In the American Revolution, Thomas Paine said, "The cause of America is the cause of all mankind." I think in 1960 the cause of all mankind is the cause of America.

Merced, California, Sept. 9, 1960

President Kennedy believed that the family farm, such as this small farm in Ohio, "should be protected and preserved as a basic American institution."

39

United States Department of Agriculture

*We have the capacity
to eliminate hunger
from the earth . . .*

Established in 1933, the Civilian
Conservation Corps was a dramatic
coupling of experimentation with
technological know-how.

So long as freedom from hunger is only half achieved, so long as two thirds of the nations have food deficits, no citizen, no nation, can afford to be satisfied. We have the ability, as members of the human race. We have the means, we have the capacity to eliminate hunger from the face of the earth in our lifetime. We need only the will. . . .

The real goal, therefore, must be to produce more food in the nations that need it. Know-how is not the problem. For the first time in the history of the world we do know how to produce enough food now to feed every man, woman and child in the world, enough to eliminate all hunger completely. Farm production has undergone a scientific revolution which is dwarfing the industrial revolution of 150 years ago, but this means that agricultural departments and ministries and governments and citizens must make a greater and more systematic effort to share this knowledge. For the first time to know how to conquer the problem and not conquer it would be a disgrace for this generation. We need to help transmit all that we know of farm technology to the ends of the earth, to overcome the barriers of ignorance and suspicion. The key to a permanent solution to world hunger is the transfer of technology which we now have to food deficit nations, and that task, second to none in importance, is the reason for this Congress.

World Food Congress, Washington, D.C., June 4, 1963

American agricultural abundance offers a great opportunity for the United States to promote the interests of peace in a significant way and to play an important role in helping to provide a more adequate diet for peoples all around the world. We must make the most vigorous and constructive use possible of this opportunity. We must narrow the gap between abundance here at home and near starvation abroad. Humanity and prudence, alike, counsel a major effort on our part.

Washington, D.C., Jan. 24, 1961

A matter of particular concern to this country must be the welfare of those who work on our farms. This is the most extraordinary miracle, this tremendous increase of our productivity since the end of World War II. It has been the most disastrous failure of the Communist system. Their effort to equal our productivity by a system of forced labor on their farms stands in very shining contrast to the tremendous increases in productivity which we have seen in the last years. The difficulty, of course, is that we have increased our productivity nearly twice as fast as we've increased our population and, therefore, our farm income has declined, our surpluses have gone up. . . .

By Telephone to a Democratic Rally
at St. Cloud, Minnesota, Oct. 7, 1962

Farm Fallacy Number One: The basic, overriding issue in agricultural policy today is the choice between flexible and rigid price supports.

This one issue alone occupies practically all of the time and attention devoted to farm problems by the Congress, the political parties, the press and the public. We give comparatively little thought to most of the truly major issues—such as the disappearance of the family-size farm, the spread between farm and consumer prices and the rising costs of the farmer's purchases. Instead we concentrate, year after year, with bitter emotional divisions, upon an issue which now has little more than symbolic value.

For the truth of the matter is that in recent years, there has been very little difference between the parties and the candidates on the question of parity price supports. . . .

Session of the American Farm Bureau Federation,
Miami Beach, Florida, Dec. 12, 1956

It is no less our purpose to insure that the farm family that produced this wealth will have a parity in income and equality in opportunity with urban families—for the family farm should be protected and preserved as a basic American institution.

Message to Congress, Washington, D.C., March 16, 1961

. . . There is a close relationship between prosperity on the farm and prosperity in the city—between the economic health of our farm community and the economic health of our nation.

Washington, D.C., Jan. 23, 1962

. . . When we talk about agriculture we should talk about it with pride and not always talk about it as one of our great problems or burdens. It is, really, one of the great success stories of the United States—and of the whole free world.

Washington, D.C., April 4, 1962

Man's great failure in the prairie, according to Secretary of the Interior Stewart L. Udall, lay in his inability to realize that "the soil was anchored to the land by grass."

National Park Service Photo:
Jack E. Boucher

Our deep spiritual confidence
compels us to invest
in the nation's future

We must reaffirm our dedication to the sound practices of conservation which can be defined as the wise use of our natural environment. . . . Our deep spiritual confidence that this nation will survive the perils of today—which may well be with us for decades to come—compels us to invest in our nation's future, to consider and meet our obligations to our children and the numberless generations that will follow.

Message to Congress, Washington, D.C., March 1, 1962

In the work of conservation, time should be made our friend, not our adversary. Actions deferred are frequently opportunities lost, and, in terms of financial outlay, dollars invested today will yield great benefits in the years to come. The progress made in the resources field in the first year of this Administration is encouraging; implementation of the new recommendations made today will maintain the momentum, enabling us to repay our debt to the past and meet our obligations to the future.

Message to Congress, Washington, D.C., March 1, 1962

I hope, in other words, that we will take this rich country of ours, given to us by God and by nature, and improve it through science and find new uses for our natural resources, to make it possible for us to sustain in this country a steadily increasing standard of living, the highest in the world, and based on that powerful fortress, to move out around the world in the defense of freedom as we have done for 18 years and as we must do in the years to come.

Great Falls, Montana, Sept. 26, 1963

In recent years, those areas of West Virginia whose economy depended on coal mining operations have suffered due to the decline in coal consumption.

National Park Service Photo: Jack E. Boucher

II

Man and the Arts

"...The wave of the future is not the conquest of the world by a single dogmatic creed but the liberation of the diverse energies of free nations and free men."

University of California, Berkeley, California, March 23, 1962

The President admired the specialized knowledge that only experts can have. But he saved his greatest confidence for the broad, generalizing human intelligence, the kind of mind that can grasp the human opportunities of the quest in space and, at the same time, realize the value of poetry to politicians. The President himself was this kind of man and he believed the only way for such men to achieve their full potential was to strive constantly toward excellence with a sense of duty and service—qualities not unrelated to the President's own life.

You can never expect a people
to be ignorant and free . . .

Thomas Jefferson once said that if you expect a people to be ignorant and free you expect what never was and never will be.

Washington, D.C., Feb. 16, 1962

Democracy is a difficult kind of government. It requires the highest qualities of self-discipline, restraint, a willingness to make commitments and sacrifices for the general interest, and also it requires knowledge.

Dublin, Ireland, June 28, 1963

. . . Knowledge is power today as never before, not only here in the United States, but the future of the free world depends in the final analysis upon the United States and upon our willingness to reach those decisions on these complicated matters which face us, with courage and clarity.

University of Wyoming, Laramie, Wyoming, Sept. 25, 1963

What I think we must realize is that the problems which now face us and their solution are far more complex, far more difficult, far more subtle, require far greater skill and discretion of judgment than any of the problems that this country has faced in its comparatively short history, or any, really, that the world has faced in its long history. The fact is that almost in the last 30 years the world of knowledge has exploded. You remember that Robert Oppenheimer said that 8 or 9 out of 10 of all the scientists who ever lived live today. This last generation has produced nearly all of the scientific breakthroughs, at least relatively, that this world of ours has ever experienced. We are alive, all of us, while this tremendous explosion of knowledge, which has expanded the horizon of our experience, so far has all taken place in the last 30 years.

University of Wyoming, Laramie, Wyoming, Sept. 25, 1963

The White House, the Washington Monument and the Jefferson Memorial are the landmarks of the nation's capital.

46

Devoney

The Land-Grant Act of 1862, by providing
Federal land for the construction
of state colleges, made possible
such fine schools as the University
of California in Berkeley.

. . . As the world presses in and knowledge presses out, the role
of the interpreter grows. Men can no longer know everything themselves; the 20th century has no universal man. All men today must
learn to know through one another—to judge across their own ignorance—to comprehend at second hand. These arts are not easily
learned. Those who would practice them must develop intensity of
perception, variety of mental activity and the habit of open concern
for truth in all its forms. Where can we expect to find a training ground
for this modern maturity, if not in our universities?

Boston College, Newton, Massachusetts, April 20, 1963

48

Men today must learn to know through one another . . .

. . . There is indeed an explosion of knowledge and its outward limits are not yet in sight. In some fields, progress seems very fast; in others, distressingly slow. It is no tribute to modern science to jump lightly to the conclusion that all its secrets of particle physics, or molecular life, or heredity, or outer space, are now within easy reach. The truth is more massive and less magical. It is that wherever we turn, in defense, in space, in medicine, in industry, in agriculture, and most of all in basic science itself, the requirement is for better work, deeper understanding, higher education. And while I have framed this comment in the terms of the natural sciences, I insist, as do all those who live in this field, that at every level of learning there must be an equal concern for history, for letters and the arts, and for man as a social being in the widest meaning of Aristotle's phrase.

Boston College, Newton, Massachusetts, April 20, 1963

There is, I know, a great tendency in every country, including my own, to consider education important but perhaps not so vital. We are so concerned in so many parts of the world with the problems that are coming today, next year, and the year after—and it does take 5 or 10 or 15 years to educate a boy or girl—and therefore there is a tendency to concentrate available resources on the problems we face now, and perhaps ignore what the potentialities and capabilities will be of our people 10 or 15 years from now.

Washington, D.C., Feb. 16, 1962

Education, quite rightly, is the responsibility of the state and the local community, but from the beginning of our country's history, from the time of the Northwest Ordinance, as John Adams and Thomas Jefferson recognized, from the time of the Morrill Act at the height of the Civil War, when the land-grant college system was set up under the Administration of President Lincoln, from the beginning it has been recognized that there must be a national commitment and that the national Government must play its role in stimulating a system of excellence which can serve the great national purpose of a free society. . . .

San Diego State College, San Diego, California, June 6, 1963

United States Department of Agriculture

It was "in the darkest and most uncertain days of the Civil War," President Kennedy noted, that Lincoln signed the act to build land-grant colleges.

49

. . . It is well to remember that this nation's first great leaders, our founders, Jefferson, Madison, Monroe, . . . Mason, Bryant and all the rest, were not only the political leaders of this country, but they were also among the most educated citizens that this country had ever produced. The two outstanding men in the 18th century, outstanding not only in the United States but in the whole Western World, were both Americans, both politicians and both philosophers and scientists, Thomas Jefferson and Benjamin Franklin.

Tacoma, Washington, Sept. 27, 1963

. . . Leadership and learning are indispensable to each other. The advancement of learning depends on community leadership for financial and political support—and the products of that learning, in turn, are essential to the leadership's hopes for continued progress and prosperity. . . .

This link between leadership and learning is not only essential at the community level. It is even more indispensable in world affairs. Ignorance and misinformation can handicap the progress of a city or a company—but they can, if allowed to prevail in foreign policy, handicap this country's security. In a world of complex and continuing problems, in a world full of frustrations and irritations, America's leadership must be guided by the lights of learning and reason—or else those who confuse rhetoric with reality and the plausible with the possible will gain the popular ascendancy with their seemingly swift and simple solutions to every world problem.

To have been delivered at Dallas, Texas, Nov. 22, 1963

Federal aid to education is not merely of importance to those with children in school. . . . We live under majority rule and if that majority is not well educated in its responsibilities, the whole nation suffers.

East Los Angeles College, Los Angeles, California, Nov. 1, 1960

. . . This university and others like it across the country, and its graduates, have recognized that these schools are not maintained by the people of the various states in order to merely give the graduates of these schools an economic advantage in the life struggle. Rather, these schools are supported by our people because our people realize that this country has needed in the past, and needs today as never before, educated men and women who are committed to the cause of freedom.

University of Washington, Seattle, Washington, Nov. 16, 1961

"It is not learning," said President Wilson, "but the spirit of service that will give a college place in the public annals of the nation. It is indispensable," he said, "if it is to do its right service, that the air of affairs should be admitted to all its classrooms . . . the air of the world's transactions, the consciousness of the solidarity of the race, the sense of the duty of man toward man . . . the promise and the hope that shine in the face of all knowledge. . . . "

Boston College, Newton, Massachusetts, April 20, 1963

. . . The Communists rest everything on the idea of a monolithic world. . . . The pursuit of knowledge, on the other hand, rests everything on the opposite idea—on the idea of a world based on diversity, self-determination, freedom.

University of California, Berkeley, California, March 23, 1962

Our aim is not simply to be first on the moon, any more than Charles Lindbergh's real aim was to be the first to Paris. His aim was to develop the techniques of our own country and other countries in the field of air and the atmosphere, and our objective in making this effort, which we hope will place one of our citizens on the moon, is to develop in a new frontier of science, commerce and cooperation, the position of the United States and the free world.

State of the Union Address to Congress,
Washington, D.C., Jan. 11, 1962

Frank O'Connor, the Irish writer, tells in one of his books how, as a boy, he and his friends would make their way across the countryside and when they came to an orchard wall that seemed too high and too doubtful to try and too difficult to permit their voyage to continue, they took off their hats and tossed them over the wall—and then they had no choice but to follow them. This nation has tossed its cap over the wall of space, and we have no choice but to follow it. Whatever the difficulties, they will be overcome; whatever the hazards, they must be guarded against. With the . . . help of all those who labor in the space endeavor, with the help and support of all Americans, we will climb this wall with safety and speed, and we shall then explore the wonders on the other side.

Dedication of Aero-Space Medical Health Center,
Brooks Air Force Base, Texas, Nov. 21, 1963

We choose to go to the moon in this decade and do the other things, not because they are easy, but because they are hard, because that goal will serve to organize and measure the best of our energies and skills, because that challenge is one that we are willing to accept, one we are unwilling to postpone, and one which we intend to win, and the others, too.

Rice University, Houston, Texas, Sept. 12, 1962

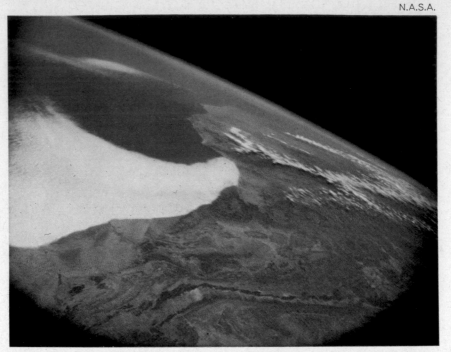

The west coast of Africa as viewed from a Mercury-Atlas space flight.

*T*he conquest of space deserves the best of all mankind . . .

We set sail on this new sea because there is new knowledge to be gained, and new rights to be won, and they must be won and used for the progress of all people. For space science, like nuclear science and all technology, has no conscience of its own. Whether it will become a force for good or ill depends on man, and only if the United States occupies a position of pre-eminence can we help decide whether this new ocean will be a sea of peace or a new terrifying theater of war. I do not say that we should or will go unprotected against the hostile misuse of space any more than we go unprotected against the hostile use of land or sea, but I do say that space can be explored and mastered without feeding the fires of war, without repeating the mistakes that man has made in extending his writ around this globe of ours.

There is no strife, no prejudice, no national conflict in outer space as yet. Its hazards are hostile to us all. Its conquest deserves the best of all mankind, and its opportunity for peaceful cooperation may never come again. But why, some say, the moon? Why choose this as our goal? And they may well ask why climb the highest mountain? Why, 35 years ago, fly the Atlantic? Why does Rice play Texas?

Rice University, Houston, Texas, Sept. 12, 1962

A vapor trail from the X-15, a rocket-propelled research plane.

N.A.S.A.

After the orbital flight of Lieut. Col. John H. Glenn Jr., President Kennedy
described him as "the kind of American of whom we are most proud."

of substantial benefit for those of us who are earthbound . . .

Many Americans make the mistake of assuming that space research has no values here on earth. Nothing could be further from the truth. Just as the wartime development of radar gave us the transistor, and all that it made possible, so research in space medicine holds the promise of substantial benefit for those of us who are earthbound, for our effort in space is not as some have suggested, a competitor for the natural resources that we need to develop the earth It is a working partner and a coproducer of these resources. And nothing makes this clearer than the fact that medicine in space is going to make our lives healthier and happier here on earth.

I give you three examples: First, medical space research may open up new understanding of man's relation to his environment. Examples of the astronaut's physical, and mental, and emotional reactions teach us more about the differences between normal and abnormal—about the causes and effects of disorientation—in metabolism which could result in extending the life span. When you study effects on our astronauts of exhaust gases which can contaminate their environment, you seek ways to alter these gases so as to reduce their toxity, you are working on problems similar to those we face in our great urban centers which themselves are being corrupted by gases and which must be clear. And second, medical space research may revolutionize the technology and the techniques of modern medicine. Whatever new devices are created, for example, to monitor our astronauts, to measure their heart activity, their breathing, their brain waves, their eye motion, at great distances, and under difficult conditions, will also represent a major advance in general medical instrumentation. Heart patients may even be able to wear a light monitor which will sound a warning if their activity exceeds certain limits. An instrument recently developed to record automatically the impact of acceleration upon an astronaut's eyes will also be of help to small children who are suffering miserably from eye defects, but are unable to describe their impairment. And also by the use of instruments similar to those used in Project Mercury, this nation's private as well as public nursing services are being improved, enabling one nurse now to give more critically ill patients greater attention than they ever could in the past.

And third, medical space research may lead to new safeguards against hazards common to many environments. Specifically, our astronauts will need fundamentally new devices to protect them from the ill effects of radiation which can have a profound influence upon medicine and man's relations to our present environment.

Dedication of Aero-Space Medical Health Center,
Brooks Air Force Base, Texas, Nov. 21, 1963

N.A.S.A.

Tiros I, the first weather satellite, launched in 1960, has helped spot major weather patterns.

If scientific discovery has not been an unalloyed blessing, if it has conferred on mankind the power not only to create but also to annihilate, it has at the same time provided humanity with a supreme challenge and a supreme testing. If the challenge and the testing are too much for humanity, then we are all doomed, but I believe that the future can be bright, and I believe it can be certain. Man is still the master of his own fate, and I believe that the power of science and the responsibility of science have offered mankind a new opportunity not only for intellectual growth but for moral discipline, not only for the acquisition of knowledge but for the strengthening of our nerve and our will.

National Academy of Sciences, Washington, D.C., Oct. 22, 1963

The United States would be willing to join with the Soviet Union and the scientists of all nations in a greater effort to make the fruits of this new knowledge available to all—and, beyond that, in an effort to extend farm technology to hungry nations—to wipe out disease—to increase the exchanges of scientists and their knowledge—and to make our own laboratories available to technicians of other lands who lack the facilities to pursue their own work. Where nature makes natural allies of us all, we can demonstrate that beneficial relations are possible even with those with whom we most deeply disagree—and this must some day be the basis of world peace and world law.

State of the Union Address to Congress, Washington, D.C., Jan. 30, 1961

As the country had reason to note in recent weeks during the debate on the Test Ban Treaty, scientists do not always unite themselves on their recommendations to the makers of policy. This is only partly because of scientific disagreements. It is even more because the big issues so often go beyond the possibilities of exact scientific determination.

National Academy of Sciences, Washington, D.C., Oct. 22, 1963

Every time you scientists make a major invention, we politicians have to invent a new institution to cope with it, and almost invariably these days and, happily, it must be an international institution. . . . The ocean, the atmosphere, outer space, belong not to one nation or one ideology, but to all mankind. . . .

National Academy of Sciences, Washington, D.C., Oct. 22, 1963

The life of the artist is stern and lonely.
He has labored hard, often amid deprivation,
to perfect his skill . . .

Today, we recognize increasingly the essentiality of artistic achievement. This is part, I think, of a nationwide movement toward excellence—a movement which had its start in the admiration of expertness and skill in our technical society, but which now demands quality in all realms of human achievement. It is part, too, of a feeling that art is the great unifying and humanizing experience . . . the side of life which expresses the emotions and embodies values and ideals of beauty.

"The Arts in America" (From the book,
Creative America, The Ridge Press, 1963)

Other countries have their national theater and opera, permanently situated in the capital and singled out for their government's special concern. Better fitted to the needs of the United States is the idea of the Cultural Center, a great stage hospitable to the best coming from this country and abroad, an institution encouraging the development of the performing arts in all their diversity of origin and variety of form. I earnestly hope that the backing of citizens across the country will make possible the fulfillment of these plans.

"The Arts in America" (From the book,
Creative America, The Ridge Press, 1963)

Too often in the past, we have thought of the artist as an idler and dilettante and of the lover of arts as somehow sissy or effete. We have done both an injustice. The life of the artist is, in relation to his work, stern and lonely. He has labored hard, often amid deprivation, to perfect his skill. He has turned aside from quick success in order to strip his vision of everything secondary or cheapening. His working life is marked by intense application and intense discipline. As for the lover of arts, it is he who, by subjecting himself to the sometimes disturbing experience of art, sustains the artist—and seeks only the reward that his life will, in consequence, be the more fully lived.

"The Arts in America" (From the book,
Creative America, The Ridge Press, 1963)

The life of the arts is a test of a nation's civilization . . .

. . . The life of the arts, far from being an interruption, a distraction, in the life of a nation, is very close to the center of a nation's purpose—and is a test of the quality of a nation's civilization.

"The Arts in America" (From the book,
Creative America, The Ridge Press, 1963)

At the same time that the creator of this painting was opening up such a wide new world to western civilization, his fellow countryman from Italy, Columbus, was opening up a new world to a new civilization. The life of this painting here before us tonight spans the entire life of that new world. We citizens of nations unborn at the time of its creation are among the inheritors and protectors of the ideals which gave it birth. For this painting is not only one of the towering achievements of the skill and vision of art, but its creator embodied the central purpose of our civilization.

Leonardo da Vinci was not only an artist and a sculptor, an architect and a scientist, and a military engineer, an occupation which he pursued, he tells us, in order to preserve the chief gift of nature, which is liberty.

In honor of the "Mona Lisa" at the National Gallery of Art,
Washington, D.C., Jan. 8, 1963

I think politicians and poets share at least one thing, and that is that their greatness depends upon the courage with which they face the challenges of life. There are many kinds of courage—bravery under fire, courage to risk reputation and friendship and career for convictions which are deeply held. Perhaps the rarest courage of all—for the skill to pursue it is given to very few men—is the courage to wage a silent battle to illuminate the nature of man and the world in which he lives. . . .

Robert Frost is often characterized as an American poet—or a New England poet. And he is, of course, all of these things, for the temper of his region and of his nation has provided a good deal of the meter and the tone in which he has dealt. But he is not a poet bounded by geography. He will live as a poet of the life of man, of the darkness and despair, as well as of the hope—which is, in his case, limited by a certain skepticism—and also for his wit and understanding of man's limitations which lie behind all of man's profoundest statements.

Recorded for the television program, "Robert Frost:
American Poet." (CBS) Feb. 26, 1961

Jacqueline Kennedy with French Ambassador Hervé Alphand and his wife (right) at the reception in honor of the "Mona Lisa."

Our national strength matters, but the spirit which informs and controls our strength matters just as much . . .

. . . Robert Frost was one of the granite figures of our time in America. He was supremely two things: an artist and an American. A nation reveals itself not only by the men it produces but also by the men it honors, the men it remembers. In America, our heroes have customarily run to men of large accomplishments. But today this college and country honors a man whose contribution was not to our size but to our spirit, not to our political beliefs but to our insight, not to our self-esteem, but to our self-comprehension. In honoring Robert Frost, we therefore can pay honor to the deepest sources of our national strength. That strength takes many forms, and the most obvious forms are not always the most significant. The men who create power make an indispensable contribution to the nation's greatness, but the men who question power make a contribution just as indispensable, especially when that questioning is disinterested, for they determine whether we use power or power uses us. Our national strength matters, but the spirit which informs and controls our strength matters just as much. This was the especial significance of Robert Frost. He brought an unsparing instinct for reality to bear on the platitudes and pieties of society. His sense of the human tragedy fortified him against self-deception and easy consolation. I have been, he wrote, one acquainted with the night. And because he knew the midnight as well as the high noon, because he understood the ordeal as well as the triumph of the human spirit, he gave his age strength with which to overcome despairs. At bottom, he held a deep faith in the spirit of man, and it is hardly an accident that Robert Frost coupled poetry and power, for he saw poetry as the means of saving power from itself. When power leads man toward arrogance, poetry reminds him of his limitations. When power narrows the areas of man concerned, poetry reminds him of the richness and diversity of his existence. When power corrupts, poetry cleanses. For art establishes the basic human truths which must serve as the touchstone of our judgment. The artist, however faithful to his personal vision of reality, becomes the last champion of the individual mind and sensibility against an intrusive society and an officious state. The great artist is thus a solitary figure. He has, as Frost said, a lover's quarrel with the world. In pursuing his perceptions of reality, he must often sail against the currents of his time. This is not a popular role. If Robert Frost was much honored during his lifetime, it was because a good many preferred to ignore his darker truths. Yet in retrospect, we see how the artist's fidelity has strengthened the fiber of our national life.

If sometimes our great artists have been the most critical of our society, it is because their sensitivity and their concern for justice which must motivate any true artist, make him aware that our nation falls short of its highest potential. I see little of more importance to the future of our country and our civilization than full recognition of the place of the artist. If art is to flourish the roots of our culture,

President Kennedy once said of the late poet Robert Frost (right), "Because of Mr. Frost's life and work . . . our hold on this planet has increased." They are pictured at a ceremony with Massachusetts Senator Leverett Saltonstall (second from left) and Secretary of the Interior Stewart L. Udall.

society must set the artist free to follow his vision wherever it takes him. We must never forget that art is not a form of propaganda; it is a form of truth. And as Mr. MacLeish once remarked of poets, there is nothing worse for our trade than to be in style. In free society art is not a weapon and it does not belong to the sphere of polemics and ideology. Artists are not engineers of the soul. It may be different elsewhere. But [in] democratic society . . . the highest duty of the writer, the composer, the artist is to remain true to himself and to let the chips fall where they may. In serving his vision of the truth, the artist best serves his nation. And the nation which disdains the mission of art invites the fate of Robert Frost's hired man, the fate of having nothing to look backward to with pride and nothing to look forward to with hope.

Amherst College, Amherst, Massachusetts, Oct. 26, 1963

61

Genius can speak at any time and the entire world will listen . . .

Ezra Stoller

An artist's conception of the grand foyer, which will overlook the Potomac River, in the Center for the Performing Arts.

. . . Today, as always, art knows no national boundaries.

Genius can speak at any time, and the entire world will hear it and listen. Behind the storm of daily conflict and crisis, the dramatic confrontations, the tumult of political struggle, the poet, the artist, the musician, continue the quiet work of centuries, building bridges of experience between peoples, reminding man of the universality of his feelings and desires and despairs, and reminding him that the forces that unite are deeper than those that divide.

Thus, art and the encouragement of art is political in the most profound sense, not as a weapon in the struggle, but as an instrument of understanding of the futility of struggle between those who share man's faith. Aeschylus and Plato are remembered today long after the triumphs of imperial Athens are gone. Dante outlived the ambitions of 13th-century Florence. Goethe stands serenely above the politics of Germany, and I am certain that after the dust of centuries has passed over our cities, we, too, will be remembered not for victories or defeats in battle or in politics, but for our contribution to the human spirit.

It was Pericles' proudest boast that, politically, Athens was the school of Hellas. If we can make our country one of the great schools of civilization, then on that achievement will surely rest our claim to the ultimate gratitude of mankind. Moreover, as a great democratic society, we have a special responsibility to the arts, for art is the great democrat calling forth creative genius from every sector of society, disregarding race or religion or wealth or color. The mere accumulation of wealth and power is available to the dictator and the democrat alike. What freedom alone can bring is the liberation of the human mind and spirit which finds its greatest flowering in the free society.

Thus, in our fulfillment of these responsibilities toward the arts lies our unique achievement as a free society.

Closed-circuit television broadcast on behalf of the National Cultural Center, Washington, D.C., Nov. 29, 1962

A model of the entrance façade of the planned John F. Kennedy Center for the Performing Arts to be built in Washington, D.C.

In 1961, the Kennedys invited cellist Pablo Casals, "one of the world's greatest artists," to give a concert at the White House.

*Societies of great creative
achievements have almost always
given a high place
to physical vigor*

I want to tell you how welcome you are to the White House. I think this is the most extraordinary collection of talent, of human knowledge, that has ever been gathered together at the White House, with the possible exception of when Thomas Jefferson dined alone.

Someone once said that Thomas Jefferson was a gentleman of 32 who could calculate an eclipse, survey an estate, tie an artery, plan an edifice, try a cause, break a horse and dance the minuet. Whatever he may have lacked, if we could have had his former colleague, Mr. Franklin, here we all would have been impressed.

Dinner honoring Nobel Prize winners of the Western
Hemisphere, Washington, D.C., April 29, 1962

It can be said with assurance of few men, in any area of human activity, that their work will long endure. William Faulkner was one of those men. Since Henry James no writer has left behind such a vast and enduring monument to the strength of American literature. His death came in Oxford, Mississippi, in the heart of the setting for that turbulent world of light and shadow which was the towering creation of his mind and art. From this world he sought to illuminate the restless searching of all men. And his insight spoke to the hearts of all who listened.

A Mississippian by birth, an American by virtue of those forces and loyalties which guided his work, a guiding citizen of our civilization by virtue of his art, William Faulkner now rests, the search done, his place secure among the great creators of this age.

On the death of William Faulkner, July 6, 1962

. . . Those societies that have produced great creative and political achievements have almost always given a high place to the physical vigor of the individual citizen. For it is only upon a foundation of individual hardiness and vitality that we can build an "exercise of vital powers along the lines of excellence."

"Physical Fitness: A Report of Progress" an
article in Look Magazine, Aug. 13, 1963

National Park Service Photo: Jack E. Boucher

Olympic National Park in Washington, a favorite with hikers,
contains some of the highest mountains of the Coast Ranges.

III

Man and His Dignity

"...We shall pay any price, bear any burden,
meet any hardship...."

Inauguration, Washington, D.C., Jan. 20, 1961

If President Kennedy becomes a romantic hero, he will be an unusual one. He was a cosmopolitan intellectual with a great respect for the facts, a deep understanding of the diverse uses of power. His temper much of the time was one of cool sophistication. Yet this was only one side of the man. Along with a slight diffidence of gesture went a smile that can only be described as boyish. In addition to his knowledge of power he was obviously a man who loved his family. Even more than he relied on facts, he felt an ultimate dependence on the human spirit, its warmth and dignity, and—as a result of struggle—its triumph even in the slums of American cities, the coal fields of West Virginia and the mud huts of Africa.

Our problems are manmade and can be solved by man...

"The real key to our national future," President Kennedy said, lies in the young people of our country.

I know few significant questions of public policy which can safely be confided to computers. In the end, the hard decisions inescapably involve imponderables of intuition, prudence and judgment.

National Academy of Sciences, Washington, D.C., Oct. 22, 1963

We can, I believe, solve a good many of our problems. I think they are manmade and they can be solved by man. And I think we must not keep our attention so fixed on those great issues of war and peace which are perhaps the most desperate and the most serious and the most important, or the great issues of space, but also concern ourselves with what happens in the United States, and particularly in those areas of the United States which have been left behind.

Northern Great Lakes Region Land and People Conference, University of Minnesota, Duluth, Minnesota, Sept. 24, 1963

. . . Peace does not rest in the charters and covenants alone. It lies in the hearts and minds of all people. And in this world out here no act, no pact, no treaty, no organization can hope to preserve it without the support and the wholehearted commitment of all people. So let us not rest all our hopes on parchment and on paper; let us strive to build peace. . . .

18th General Assembly of the United Nations, New York, New York, Sept. 20, 1963

It is my judgment that there is no career that could possibly be open to you in the 1960s that will offer to you as much satisfaction, as much stimulus, as little compensation perhaps financially, as being a servant of the United States Government.

I think within all of us, and really in a sense, I suppose endowed almost by nature in addition to a natural desire to advance our own interests, there is also a parallel desire, and that is to be part of this great enterprise of public service. The totalitarian powers have exploited that. Even in Cuba Mr. Castro's emphasis, certainly at the beginning, was on a desire to improve the lot of the Cuban people. In China we had all of these examples of people spending their days off going out on illiteracy, health, building dams, doing all the things to build a better country. This is in all of us.

I think that it is a more difficult and subtle problem in a democracy, with a great deal of emphasis, of course, on individual liberty, on the right of pursuing our private interests, and so on, so that while there is this desire, frequently it does not have a chance to express itself. But the desire is there. . . .

To Participants in the Summer Intern Program for College Students, Washington, D. C., June 20, 1962

. . . The overseas success of our Peace Corps volunteers, most of them young men and women carrying skills and ideals to needy people, suggests the merits of a similar corps serving our own community needs: in mental hospitals, on Indian reservations, in centers for the aged or for young delinquents, in schools for the illiterate or the handicapped. As the idealism of our youth has served world peace, so can it serve the domestic tranquillity.

State of the Union Address to Congress,
Washington, D.C., Jan. 14, 1963

We are politicians in the sense that we believe political action through one of the political parties . . . is the best means of achieving service for our country. . . . These matters do not end on election day. All this is a means to an end, not an end in itself, and the end is service to our country. . . .

Jefferson-Jackson Day Brunch,
Middletown, Ohio, Oct. 17, 1960

I know that many Foreign Service officers feel (like former Marines, who believe that the old days were the best days) that the days before World War II were the golden days of the Foreign Service, that since then the Foreign Service has fallen on hard times and that there is a good deal of uncertainty about what the future may bring.

I would like to differ with that view completely. In my opinion, today, as never before, is the golden period of the Foreign Service.

In the days before the war, we dealt with a few countries and a few leaders. I remember what Ambassador Dawes said, that the job was hard on the feet and easy on the brain. Theodore Roosevelt talked about those who *resided* in the Foreign Service rather than working in it. We were an isolationist country, by tradition and by policy and by statute. And therefore those of you who lived in the Foreign Service led a rather isolated life, dealing with comparatively few people, uninvolved in the affairs of this country or in many ways in the affairs of the country to which you may have been accredited.

That is all changed now. The power and influence of the United States are involved in the national life of dozens of countries that did not exist before 1945, many of which are so hard pressed.

This is the great period of the Foreign Service, much greater than any period that has gone before. And it will be so through this decade, and perhaps even more in the years to come, if we are able to maintain ourselves with success.

But it places the heaviest burdens upon all of you. Instead of becoming merely experts in diplomatic history, or in current clippings from The New York Times, now you have to involve yourselves in every element of foreign life—labor, the class struggle, cultural affairs and all the rest—attempting to predict in what direction the forces will move. The Ambassador has to be the master of all these things, as well as knowing his own country. Now you have to know

Mr. Kennedy and his sister Mrs. Eunice Shriver greet a volunteer for the German Development Service, a group similar to the Peace Corps.

Only the best education enables the great mass of people to make intelligent judgments, the President told the Fulbright exchange teachers.

"It is my task to *report* the state of
the Union," President Kennedy said;
"to *improve* it is the task of us all."

The President and Mrs. Kennedy, the
Vice President and Mrs. Johnson, and
Congressional leaders at the 1962
Congressional Reception.

all about the United States, every facet of its life, all the great reforms of the thirties, the forties and the fifties, if you are going to represent the United States powerfully and with strength and with vigor. When you represent the United States today, it is not a question of being accredited to a few people whose tenure is certain, but instead, of making predictions about what will be important events, what will be the elements of power or the elements of struggle, and which way we should move. And this calls for the finest judgment.

Meeting of the American Foreign Service Association,
Washington, D.C., May 31, 1962

Members of the Congress, the Constitution makes us not rivals for power but partners for progress. We are all trustees for the American people, custodians of the American heritage. It is my task to *report* the state of the Union—to *improve* it is the task of us all.

State of the Union Address to Congress,
Washington, D.C., Jan. 11, 1962

About 35 years ago, a Congressman from California who had just been elected received a letter from an irate constituent which said: "During the campaign you promised to have the Sierra Madre Mountains reforested. You have been in office one month and you haven't done so."

Fort Worth Chamber of Commerce,
Fort Worth, Texas, Nov. 22, 1963

. . . The Federal Government is not a remote bureaucracy. It must seek to meet those needs of the individual, the family and the community which can best be met by the nationwide cooperation of all, and which cannot be met by state and local governments.

These needs must be met—and to take them out of the Federal budget will only cast them on state and local governments, whose expenditures, debt and payrolls have all increased many times faster than those of the Federal Government.

. . . If it were not for Federal aid to hard-pressed state and local governments, the Federal cash budget today would be in balance. The Federal Government is the people, and the budget is a reflection of their needs. As the nation grows larger, so does the budget, but nondefense budget expenditures are lower now in relation to our gross national product, roughly seven per cent, than they were 25 years ago.

Convention of American Society of
Newspaper Editors, Washington, D.C., April 19, 1963

. . . There isn't any doubt that the center of action in the American constitutional system is the President of the United States. The Constitution places the greatest responsibility for the conduct of our foreign affairs, particularly, upon the President, and unless the President of the United States speaks for the nation, unless the Presi-

70

dent of the United States is able to personify the force of the nation, then the nation does not move ahead, does not move to accomplish its unfinished business, does not give an image of vitality and strength throughout the world.

Philadelphia, Pennsylvania, Oct. 29, 1960

When I ran for the Presidency of the United States, I knew that this country faced serious challenges, but I could not realize—nor could any man realize who does not bear the burdens of this office—how heavy and constant would be those burdens. . . .

Television-Radio Address,
Washington, D.C., July 25, 1961

The other point is something that President Eisenhower said to me on January 19th. He said, "There are no easy matters that will ever come to you as President. If they are easy, they will be settled at a lower level." So that the matters that come to you as President are always the difficult matters, and matters that carry with them large implications. So this contributes to some of the burdens of the office of the Presidency, which other Presidents have commented on.

Television-Radio Interview: "After Two Years—A Conversation
with the President," Washington, D.C., Dec. 17, 1962

. . . I think, of course, great times make great Presidents and great men. . . . A sense of the future and the past and a wide cultural experience which makes it possible for them to draw on the lives of other men and the experiences of other men and apply it to a particular situation, moral courage, a sense of the future, a sense of the past, a physical vitality, intellectual vitality, intellectual curiosity and purpose. I would say those are the qualities.

Television-Radio Debate, Chicago, Illinois, Sept. 26, 1960

Nor is it accidental that many of our outstanding Presidents, men such as Jefferson or Wilson or Truman, have had a deep sense of history. For all of the disciplines, the study of the folly and achievements of man is best calculated to help develop the critical sense of what is permanent and meaningful amid the mass of superficial and transient events and decisions which engulf the Presidency. And it is on this sense, more than any other, that great leadership depends.

"John F. Kennedy Tells Youth How to Prepare for the Presidency,"
an article in Parade Magazine, Sept. 23, 1962

The newspaper headlines and the television screens give us a short view. They so flood us with the stop-press details of daily stories that we lose sight of one of the great movements of history. Yet it is the profound tendencies of history and not the passing excitements, that will shape our future.

University of California, Berkeley, California, March 23, 1962

Great times make great Presidents...

Cornell Capa: Magnum

" . . . The matters that come to you as President are always the difficult matters," Mr. Kennedy said. Lyndon B. Johnson is pictured in the foreground.

We love our country for what it someday will be...

"Today, in the world of freedom, the proudest boast is '*Ich bin ein Berliner,*'" Mr. Kennedy told a cheering crowd in West Berlin.

... Though we like to think of ourselves as a young country—this is the oldest republic in the world. When the United States was founded there was a King in France, and a Czar in Russia, and an Emperor in Peking. They have all been wiped away, but the United States has still survived.

Inaugural Anniversary Dinner, Washington, D.C., Jan. 20, 1962

The theory of independence is as old as man himself, and it was not invented in this hall.* But it was in this hall that the theory became a practice; that the word went out to all, and Thomas Jefferson's phrase, that "the God who gave us life, gave us liberty at the same time."
*Independence Hall

Philadelphia, Pennsylvania, July 4, 1962

In my own home city of Boston, Faneuil Hall—once the meeting place of the authors of the American Revolution—has long been known as the "cradle of American liberty." But when, in 1852, the Hungarian patriot Kossuth addressed an audience there, he criticized its name. "It is," he said, "a great name—but there is something in it which saddens my heart. You should not say 'American liberty.' You should say 'liberty in America.' Liberty should not be either American or European—it should just be 'liberty.'"

Kossuth was right. For unless liberty flourishes in all lands, it cannot flourish in one. Conceived in one hall, it must be carried out in many.

Frankfurt, Germany, June 25, 1963

The world of Calhoun, the world of Taft had its own hard problems and notable challenges. But its problems are not our problems. Their age is not our age. As every past generation has had to disenthrall itself from an inheritance of truisms and stereotypes, so in our own time we must move on from the reassuring repetition of stale phrases to a new, difficult, but essential confrontation with reality.

... The great enemy of the truth is very often not the lie—deliberate, contrived and dishonest—but the myth—persistent, persuasive and unrealistic.

Yale University, New Haven, Connecticut, June 11, 1962

... We love our country, not for what it was, though it has always been great—not for what it is, though of this we are deeply proud—but for what it someday can and, through the efforts of us all, someday will be.

Meeting of the National Industrial Conference Board, Washington, D.C., February 13, 1961

There will always be dissident voices heard in the land, expressing opposition without alternatives, finding fault but never favor, perceiving gloom on every side and seeking influence without responsibility. Those voices are inevitable.

But today other voices are heard in the land—voices preaching doctrines wholly unrelated to reality, wholly unsuited to the sixties, doctrines which apparently assume that words will suffice without weapons, that vituperation is as good as victory and that peace is a sign of weakness. At a time when the national debt is steadily being reduced in terms of its burden on our economy, they see that debt as the greatest single threat to our security. At a time when we are steadily reducing the number of Federal employes serving every thousand citizens, they fear those supposed hordes of civil servants far more than the actual hordes of opposing armies.

We cannot expect that everyone, to use the phrase of a decade ago, will "talk sense to the American people." But we can hope that fewer people will listen to nonsense. And the notion that this nation is headed for defeat through deficit, or that strength is but a matter of slogans, is nothing but just plain nonsense.

> To have been delivered to Dallas Citizens Council, Dallas
> Assembly and the Graduate Research Center of the
> Southwest, Dallas, Texas, Nov. 22, 1963

It is in times such as these that many men, weak in courage and frail in nerve, develop the tendency to turn suspiciously on their neighbors and leaders. Unable to face up to the dangers from without, they become convinced that the real danger is from within.

> Washington, D.C., June 22, 1962

. . . I think the American people expect more from us than cries of indignation and attack. The times are too grave, the challenge too urgent, the stakes too high to permit the customary passions of political debate. We are not here to curse the darkness, but to light the candle that can guide us through that darkness to a safe and sane future. As Winston Churchill said on taking office some 20 years ago: If we open a quarrel between the present and the past, we shall be in danger of losing the future. . . . Today our concern must be with that future. For the world is changing. The old era is ending. The old ways will not do. . . .

> Acceptance of nomination, Los Angeles, California, July 15, 1960

We shall be judged more by what we do at home than by what we preach abroad. . . . These domestic tasks do not divert our energy or our security—they provide the very foundation for freedom's survival and success.

> State of the Union Address to Congress,
> Washington, D.C., Jan. 14, 1963

White House Photo: Abbie Rowe

Mothers may want their sons to grow up to be President, Mr. Kennedy said, but they do not want them to become politicians in the process.

America is ready to move from self-indulgence to self-denial...

We are a blessed land. More American citizens are working than at any time in our history, earning more and producing the highest volume of goods and services on record. . . .

These achievements have been the work of men. They are the result of challenges faced, problems confronted and effort expended, sometimes at great personal cost. They have been earned first and then inherited by our own generation. We must keep that same faith with our own children.

Labor Day Message, Newport, Rhode Island, Sept. 3, 1962

. . . I believe that America is ready to move from self-indulgence to self-denial. It will take will and effort. But I believe that America is ready to work. It will take vision and boldness. But I believe that America is still bold.

Hyde Park, New York, Aug. 14, 1960

We all believe in the free enterprise system and the competition in the market place, and we believe from that competition comes the advancement of the general interest from the clash of private interests and public interests to serve. But I don't think we can merely sell it, nor have we historically, the idea that competitive factors will protect completely the public interests. If we felt that, we never would have had an Antitrust Division or a Federal Trade Commission, or many of the other agencies and there would not be the present need for the action by the Congress and executive. So we want private enterprise to function effectively, and I think it is our job to assist by making it difficult for those who seek to defraud, those who are less concerned about safety, those who seem to exploit the private enterprise system, in a sense, by being less responsible. In this I think this council is most important.

Consumers' Advisory Council, Washington, D.C., July 19, 1962

Fifty years or so ago the American labor movement was little more than a group of dreamers, and look at it now. Nearly 14 million men and women belong to unions affiliated with the AFL-CIO. From coast to coast, in factories, stores, warehouses and business establishments of all kinds, industrial democracy is at work. Employes, represented by free and democratic trade unions of their own choosing, participate actively in determining their wages, hours and working conditions. Their living standards are the highest in the world. Their job rights are protected by collective bargaining agreements. They have fringe benefits that were unheard of less than a generation ago. Is there any better monument to the unlimited ability of Americans to turn dreams to reality than the American labor movement?

By telephone to the New York State AFL-CIO, Aug. 30, 1960

74

During the past six years the level of unemployment has remained far too high. Men have been without jobs and factories have been without orders, primarily because the over-all level of market demand has fallen short of the nation's productive capacity. But when job opportunities are already scarce, those whom technological progress or industrial change displace are more likely than ever to join the ranks of the unemployed than to find a new job. General unemployment is thus a double burden; as it penalizes those without jobs, it also creates fear and resentment against the very kind of modernization and change upon which our economic progress must in the long run depend.

. . . Seen through the magnifying lens of our general unemployment problem of the past six years, the difficulties faced by those who are technologically and structurally displaced from work have captured unprecedented attention; and this is as it should be. Our awareness has been mounting that it is unfair to ask particular workers—or in some instances, even particular employers—to bear the full social costs that attend such progress.

Message on Railroad Rules Dispute,
Washington, D.C., July 22, 1963

Some people may think it strange that jobs, which was the great issue of the thirties, when we were in a depression, should also be the great concern of the sixties, when we enjoy a relative period of economic prosperity. The difficulty in the thirties was that there was an inordinately low supply of jobs for the men and women who wished to find work.

The difficulty now is the tremendously high manpower demand which exceeds the supply of jobs.

Chicago, Illinois, March 23, 1963

We believe that if men have the talent to invent new machines that put men out of work, they have the talent to put those men back to work. . . .

Wheeling, West Virginia, Sept. 27, 1962

I know that those of you who are vitally interested in American Indians are not concerned only with the extraordinary past but also the present and the future and the opportunities which are going to be available to the younger American Indians who will be coming along who we want to live very fruitful lives.

In your Chicago declaration, you reiterated—which of course was unnecessary—your strong love for this country of which you are the first citizens. So I hope that this visit here which is more than ceremonial will be a reminder to all Americans of the number of Indians whose housing is inadequate, whose education is inadequate,

The President's Committee on Employment of the Handicapped presents its new seal to Mr. Kennedy.

The President confers with his brother and adviser, Attorney General Robert Kennedy, at the White House.

75

whose employment is inadequate, whose health is inadequate, whose security and old age is inadequate—a very useful reminder that there is still a good deal of unfinished business.

To Delegates from the American Indian Chicago
Conference, Washington, D.C., Aug. 15, 1962

A new, enlightened policy of immigration need not provide for unlimited immigration but simply for so much immigration as our country could absorb and which would be in the national interest —the most serious defect in the present law is not that it is restrictive but that many of the restrictions are based on false or unjust premises. We must avoid what the Massachusetts poet John Boyle O'Reilly once called:

Organized charity, scrimped and iced,
In the name of a cautious, statistical Christ.

Such a policy should be generous; it should be fair; it should be flexible. With such a policy we could turn to the world with clean hands and a clear conscience.

"A Nation of Immigrants," a pamphlet
by Senator John F. Kennedy, 1959

In 1921, Congress passed and the President signed the first major law in our country's history severely limiting new immigration. An era in American history has ended and we were committed to a radically new policy toward the peopling of the nation. . . . The famous words of Emma Lazarus on the pedestal of the Statue of Liberty read: "Give me your tired, your poor, your huddled masses yearning to breathe free." Under present law it is suggested that there should be added: "as long as they come from Northern Europe, are not too tired or too poor or slightly ill, never stole a loaf of bread, never joined any questionable organization, and can document their activities for the past two years."

"A Nation of Immigrants," a pamphlet
by Senator John F. Kennedy, 1959

This is not a sectional issue. Difficulties over segregation and discrimination exist in every city, in every state of the Union, producing in many cities a rising tide of discontent that threatens the public safety.

Nor is this a partisan issue. In a time of domestic crisis, men of good will and generosity should be able to unite regardless of party or politics.

This is not even a legal or legislative issue alone. It is better to settle these matters in the courts than on the streets, and new laws are needed at every level. But law alone cannot make men see right.

We are confronted primarily with a moral issue. It is as old as the Scriptures and is as clear as the American Constitution. The heart

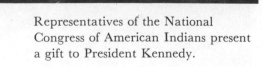

Representatives of the National Congress of American Indians present a gift to President Kennedy.

76

of the question is whether all Americans are to be afforded equal rights and equal opportunities, whether we are going to treat our fellow Americans as we want to be treated.

If an American, because his skin is dark, cannot eat lunch in a restaurant open to the public, if he cannot send his children to the best public school available, if he cannot vote for the public officials who represent him, if, in short, he cannot enjoy the full and free life which all of us want, then who among us would be content to have the color of his skin changed and stand in his place?

Television-Radio Address, Washington, D.C., June 11, 1963

... It is hard for any nation to focus on an external or subversive threat to its independence when its energies are drained in daily combat with the forces of poverty and despair. It makes little sense for us to assail, in speeches and resolutions, the horrors of Communism, to spend $50 billion a year to prevent its military advance—and then to begrudge spending, largely on American products, less than one tenth of that amount to help other nations strengthen their independence and cure the social chaos in which Communism always has thrived.

State of the Union Address to Congress, Washington, D.C., Jan. 14, 1963

... The Emancipation Proclamation was not an end. It was a beginning. The century since has seen the struggle to convert freedom from rhetoric to reality. It has been in many respects a somber story. . . . Despite humiliation and deprivation, the Negro retained his loyalty to the United States and to democratic institutions. He showed this loyalty by brave service in two world wars, by the rejection of extreme or violent policies, by a quiet and proud determination to work for long-denied rights within the framework of the American Constitution.

Emancipation Day Message, Washington, D.C., Sept. 22, 1962

If a Negro baby is born—and this is true also of Puerto Ricans and Mexicans in some of our cities—he has about one half as much chance to get through high school as a white baby. He has one third as much chance to get through college as a white student. He has about a third as much chance to be a professional man, and about half as much chance to own a house. He has about four times as much chance that he'll be out of work in his life as the white baby. I think we can do better.

Television-Radio Debate, Chicago, Illinois, Sept. 26, 1960

Despite humiliation the Negro has remained loyal...

U.S.I.A.

Senator Kennedy talks with delegates to the New York Herald Tribune Forum in 1957 at a Washington, D.C., luncheon.

77

People everywhere
look to the splendor
of our ideals...

White House Photo: Abbie Rowe

"It ought to be possible,"
Mr. Kennedy said, "for every American
to enjoy the privileges of being American
without regard to his race or his color."

Civil rights are not merely of importance to minority groups. If the full rights of our Constitution, the full values of human dignity, are not available to every American, then they no longer have the same meaning for any American. They no longer have the same appeal to those in other lands of other races and religions, and they are a majority whose respect we seek. And they no longer guarantee us a nation that draws upon the full talents of every citizen. We do not want a Negro who could be a doctor, in a city short of doctors, working as a messenger.

East Los Angeles College, Los Angeles, California, Nov. 1, 1960

... We must recognize that older people have a right to decent food, clothing, housing; a right to a decent income; a right, earned by a lifetime of useful service, to live out their lives in useful, satisfying, continued service to their world and to those who love them.

In the richest country in the world, this is not too much to ask—for those who made it rich.

Reading, Pennsylvania, Sept. 16, 1960

I think we ought to look, as a society, at what our women are doing and the opportunities before them. Other societies, which we don't admire as much as our own, it seems to me, have given this problem particular attention.

Washington, D.C., Oct. 11, 1963

Looking at all you ladies and seeing what you have done with some of your distinguished officeholders, I recall an experience of the suffragettes who picketed the White House back during the First World War. The leader of the suffragettes was arrested. As she was taken away in a truck, she turned to her girls and said, "Don't worry, girls. Pray to the Lord. She will protect you."

Breakfast of Women's Division of Democratic State Central
Committee of California, Hollywood, California, June 8, 1963

... I have found—as I am sure you have, in your travels—that people everywhere, in spite of occasional disappointments, look to us—not to our wealth or power, but to the splendor of our ideals. For our nation is commissioned by history to be either an observer of freedom's failure or the cause of its success. Our overriding obligation in the months ahead is to fulfill the world's hopes by fulfilling our own faith.

State of the Union Address to Congress,
Washington, D.C., Jan. 11, 1962

I don't think the American people realize how extraordinary has been our responsibility, and how extraordinary has been our effort. To attempt to maintain the freedom of dozens of countries,

30 or 40 of which are newly independent in the last few years, with limited traditions, with a limited number of educated people, to try to maintain the balance of power against a monolithic Communist apparatus, was an assignment which challenged even the resources, the wealth and the experience and the dedication of our own people. There have been some disappointments and some defeats. But it seems to me, all in all, as we look at the world, however imperfect it may be, however frustrating it may be, however limited our authority may be on occasions, however impossible we may find it to have our writ accepted, nevertheless, the United States is secure, it is at peace, and a good many dozen of countries are secure because of us.

This was a policy carried out through three Administrations of different parties, but I think every American citizen, 180 million of them, can take satisfaction in that record.

Northern Great Lakes Region Land and People Conference,
University of Minnesota, Duluth, Minnesota, Sept. 24, 1963

We cannot escape our dangers—neither must we let them drive us into panic or narrow isolation. In many areas of the world where the balance of power already rests with our adversaries, the forces of freedom are sharply divided. It is one of the ironies of our time that the techniques of a harsh and repressive system should be able to instill discipline and ardor in its servants—while the blessings of liberty have too often stood for privilege, materialism and a life of ease.

But I have a different view of liberty.

State of the Union Address to Congress,
Washington, D.C., Jan. 30, 1961

The hour of decision has arrived. We cannot afford to "wait and see what happens," while the tide of events sweeps over and beyond us. We must use time as a tool, not as a couch.

National Association of Manufacturers,
New York, New York, Dec. 6, 1961

. . . We must face the fact that the United States is neither omnipotent or omniscient—that we are only six per cent of the world's population—that we cannot impose our will upon the other 94 per cent of mankind—that we cannot right every wrong or reverse each adversity—and that therefore there cannot be an American solution to every world problem.

University of Washington, Seattle, Washington, Nov. 16, 1961

It is just and fitting, and appropriate and traditional, that I should come here to Canada—across a border that knows neither guns nor guerrillas.

But we share more than a common border. We share a common

N.A.A.C.P.

Discrimination is not a sectional issue, the President said; it is a moral issue.

Peace Corps Photo

A Peace Corps volunteer teaches a primary school physical education class in British Honduras.

79

*Our greatest
challenge lies beyond
the cold war...*

heritage, traced back to those early settlers who traveled from the beachheads of the Maritime Provinces and New England to the far reaches of the Pacific Coast. Henry Thoreau spoke a common sentiment for them all: "Eastward I go only by force, westward I go free. I must walk toward Oregon and not toward Europe." We share common values from the past, a common defense line at present, and common aspirations for the future—our future, and indeed the future of all mankind.

Geography has made us neighbors. History has made us friends. Economics has made us partners. And necessity has made us allies. Those whom nature hath so joined together, let no man put asunder.

Canadian Parliament, Ottawa, Canada, May 17, 1961

This hemisphere is our home and I cannot understand . . . why it is possible for the Soviet Union with one half of the wealth of the United States to put as much resources and money and assistance into the single island of Cuba of six million people as this rich country does in its own back yard for all of the countries of Latin America.

Convention of the AFL-CIO, New York, New York, Nov. 15, 1963

No Cuban need feel trapped between dependence on the broken promises of foreign Communism and the hostility of the rest of the hemisphere, for once Cuban sovereignty has been restored we will extend the hand of friendship and assistance to a Cuba whose political and economic institutions have been shaped by the will of the Cuban people.

Inter-American Press Association,
Miami Beach, Florida, Nov. 18, 1963

U.S.I.S.

Contrary to the assertions of Soviet Premier Khrushchev, Mr. Kennedy said, the family of man can accept differences of ideology and economics.

. . . We must not forget that our Alliance for Progress is more than a doctrine of development—a blueprint of economic advance. Rather it is an expression of the noblest goals of our society. It says that want and despair need not be the lot of free men. . . . It says that material progress is meaningless without individual freedom and political liberty. It is a doctrine of the freedom of man in the most spacious sense of that freedom.

Reception for Latin American Diplomats,
Washington, D.C., March 13, 1962

The great battleground for the defense and expansion of freedom today is the whole southern half of the globe—Asia, Latin America, Africa and the Middle East—the lands of the rising peoples. Their revolution is the greatest in human history. They seek an end to injustice, tyranny and exploitation. More than an end, they seek a beginning.

And theirs is a revolution which we would support regardless of the cold war, and regardless of which political or economic route they should choose to freedom.

For the adversaries of freedom did not create the revolution; nor did they create the conditions which compel it. But they are seeking to ride the crest of its wave—to capture it for themselves.

Message to Congress, Washington, D.C., May 25, 1961

. . . The blessings of life have not been distributed evenly to the family of man. Life expectancy in this most fortunate of nations has reached the Biblical three score years and ten; but in the less developed nations of Africa, Asia and Latin America, the overwhelming majority of infants cannot expect to live even two score years and five. In those vast continents, more than half the children of primary school age are not in school. More than half the families live in substandard dwellings. More than half the people live on less than $100 a year. Two out of every three adults are illiterate.

The family of man can survive differences of race and religion. Contrary to the assertions of Mr. Khrushchev, it can accept differences of ideology, politics and economics. But it cannot survive in the form in which we know it a nuclear war—and neither can it long endure the growing gulf between the rich and the poor.

Protestant Council, New York, New York, Nov. 8, 1963

If a free society cannot help the many who are poor, it cannot save the few who are rich.

Inauguration, Washington, D.C., Jan. 20, 1961

Our greatest challenge is still the world that lies beyond the cold war. . . .

State of the Union Address to Congress, Washington, D.C., Jan. 30, 1961

Justice cannot wait for too many meetings. It cannot wait for the action of the Congress or the courts. We face a moment of moral and constitutional crisis, and men of generosity and vision must make themselves heard in every section of this country. I do not say that all men are equal in their ability, their character or their motivation, but I say they should be equal in their chance to develop their character, their motivation and their ability. They should be given a fair chance to develop all the talents which they have, which is a basic assumption and presumption of this democracy of ours.

U.S. Conference of Mayors, Honolulu, Hawaii, June 9, 1963

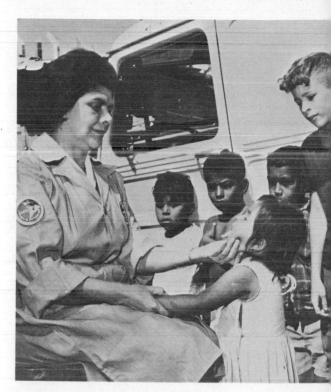

A nurse, a member of a mobile health team sponsored by the Alliance for Progress, examines children in a remote village in El Salvador.

There is no reason why people in this hemisphere should live on an inadequate diet, the President told Latin American farm leaders.

*Let history record
that we took the first
step toward peace...*

I would remind those who ask that question, including those in other small countries, of these words of one of the great orators of the English language:

"All the world owes much to the little 'five feet high' nations. The greatest art of the world was the work of little nations. The most enduring literature of the world came from little nations. The heroic deeds that thrill humanity through generations were the deeds of little nations fighting for their freedom. And, oh, yes, the salvation of mankind came through a little nation."

Joint Session of the Dáil and Seanad, Eireann,
Dublin, Ireland, June 28, 1963

About 50 years ago, an Irishman from New Ross traveled down to Washington with his family and, in order to tell his neighbors how well he was doing, he had his picture taken in front of the White House and said, "This is our summer home. Come and see us." Well, it is our home also in the winter, and I hope you will come and see us.

New Ross, Ireland, June 27, 1963

There are many kinds of strength and no one kind will suffice. . . . Above all, words alone are not enough. The United States is a peaceful nation. And where our strength and determination are clear, our words need merely to convey conviction, not belligerence. If we are strong, our strength will speak for itself. If we are weak, words will be of no help. . . . It was not the Monroe Doctrine that kept all Europe away from this hemisphere—it was the strength of the British fleet and the width of the Atlantic Ocean. It was not General Marshall's speech at Harvard which kept Communism out of Western Europe—it was the strength and stability made possible by our military and economic assistance. . . . Our successful defense of freedom was due—not to the words we used—but to the strength we stood ready to use on behalf of the principles we stand ready to defend.

To have been delivered at Dallas, Texas, Nov. 22, 1963

My fellow citizens: Let no one doubt that this is a difficult and dangerous effort on which we have set out. No one can foresee precisely what course it will take or what cost or casualties will be incurred. Many months of sacrifice and self-discipline lie ahead—months in which both our patience and our will will be tested—months in which many threats and denunciations will keep us aware of our dangers. But the greatest danger of all would be to do nothing.

The path we have chosen for the present is full of hazards, as all paths are—but it is the one most consistent with our character and courage as a nation and our commitments around the world. The cost of freedom is always high—but Americans have always paid it. And one path we shall never choose, and that is the path of surrender or submission.

Our goal is not the victory of might, but the vindication of right—not peace at the expense of freedom, but both peace *and*

Ireland, which made President Kennedy feel "so very much at home" during his 1963 visit, honored him in death by sending a troop of 26 young Irish cadets to his funeral.

84

freedom, here in this hemisphere, and, we hope, around the world. God willing, that goal will be achieved.

Television-Radio Address on the Soviet Arms
Buildup in Cuba, Washington, D.C., Oct. 22, 1962

So let us begin anew—remembering on both sides that civility is not a sign of weakness, and sincerity is always subject to proof. Let us never negotiate out of fear. But let us never fear to negotiate. . . .

All this will not be finished in the first 100 days. Nor will it be finished in the first 1,000 days, nor in the life of this Administration, nor even perhaps in our lifetime on this planet. But let us begin.

Inauguration, Washington, D.C., Jan. 20, 1961

. . . To adopt a black and white, all or nothing policy subordinates our interest to our irritations.

Salt Lake City, Utah, Sept. 26, 1963

It is rarely possible to recapture missed opportunities to achieve a more secure and peaceful world. To govern is to choose. . . .

Message to Senate, Washington, D.C., Aug. 8, 1963

. . . In the next 20 years . . . the choices we present to the world will be more difficult, and for some the future will seem even more empty of hope and progress. The barrage upon truth will grow more constant, and some people cannot bear the responsibility of a free choice which goes with self-government. And finally, shrinking from choice, they turn to those who prevent them from choosing, and thus find in a kind of prison, a kind of security.

Anniversary of the Voice of America, Washington, D.C., Feb. 26, 1962

I have faith that the human race can make its way through the treacherous mine field represented by the arms race in weapons of mass destruction. If it is to do so, however, American political leaders must not mistake slogans and discourtesy for strength, and Russian political leaders would be well advised to avoid the same error.

Review of a book, *Deterrent or Defense* by
B. H. Liddell Hart, in Saturday Review, Sept. 3, 1960

. . . Now, for the first time in many years, the path of peace may be open. No one can be certain what the future will bring. No one can say whether the time has come for an easing of the struggle. But history and our own conscience will judge us harsher if we do not now make every effort to test our hopes by action, and this is the place to begin. According to the ancient Chinese proverb, "A journey of a thousand miles must begin with a single step."

My fellow Americans, let us take that first step. Let us, if we can, get back from the shadows of war and seek out the way of peace. And if that journey is 1000 miles, or even more, let history record that we, in this land, at this time, took the first step.

Television-Radio Address, Washington, D.C., July 26, 1963

White House Photo Abbie Rowe

The strongest insurance for the defense of Europe, the President told West German Chancellor Konrad Adenauer, is the close tie between the Federal Republic and the United States.

The Test Ban Treaty does not end our competition with Communism

White House Photo: Abbie Rowe

Mr. Kennedy addresses the 11th Annual Presidential Prayer Breakfast at which the Reverend Billy Graham (right) was a guest.

White House Photo: Abbie Rowe

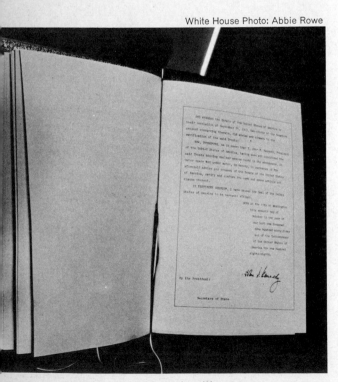

"If this treaty fails, it will not be our doing," President Kennedy said as he signed the Nuclear Test Ban Treaty.

I do not believe that the Test Ban Treaty means that the competition between the Communist system and ourselves will end. What we hope is that it will not be carried into the sphere of nuclear war. But the competition will go on. Which society is the most productive? Which society educates its children better? Which society maintains a higher rate of economic growth? Which society produces more cultural and intellectual stimulus? Which society, in other words, is the happier?

Great Falls, Montana, Sept. 26, 1963

If this treaty fails, it will not be our doing, and even if it fails, we shall not regret that we have made this clear and honorable national commitment to the cause of man's survival.

At the signing of the Nuclear Test Ban Treaty, Washington, D.C., Oct. 7, 1963

This country was founded by men and women who were dedicated or came to be dedicated to two propositions: first, a strong religious conviction, and, secondly, a recognition that this conviction could flourish only under a system of freedom.

I think it is appropriate that we pay tribute to this great constitutional principle which is enshrined in the First Amendment of the Constitution: the principle of religious independence, of religious liberty, of religious freedom. But I think it is also important that we pay tribute and acknowledge another great principle, and that is the principle of religious conviction. Religious freedom has no significance unless it is accompanied by conviction. And therefore the Puritans and the Pilgrims of our own section of New England, the Quakers of Pennsylvania, the Catholics of Maryland, the Presbyterians of North Carolina, the Methodists and the Baptists who came later, all shared these two great traditions. . . .

Dedication Breakfast of International Christian Leadership, Washington, D.C., Feb. 9, 1961

I believe yesterday we saw an interesting contrast in the response which Colonel Glenn made as to whether he had prayed, and he said that he had not, that he had made his peace with his Maker many years before, and the statement made by Titov in which during his flight, as he flew over the Soviet Union he realized, he said, the wonders of the Communist system.

I preferred Colonel Glenn's answer because I thought it was so solidly based, in his own life, in his activities in his church, and I think reflects a quality which we like to believe and I think we can believe is much a part of our American heritage. . . .

Presidential Prayer Breakfast, Washington, D.C., March 1, 1962

With a good conscience our only sure reward, with history the final judge of our deeds, let us go forth to lead the land we love, asking His blessing and His help, but knowing that here on earth God's work must truly be our own.

Inauguration, Washington, D.C., Jan. 20, 1961

Epilogue

"...This is a time for courage and a time of challenge. Neither conformity nor complacency will do. Neither the fanatics nor the fainthearted are needed.... Let us stand together with renewed confidence in our cause...."

To have been delivered at Austin, Texas, Nov. 22, 1963

Then the President, the father and husband, the man so ardently involved and alive was dead. To that first Day of Infamy—December 7, 1941—a generation of Americans now added a second: November 22, 1963. And for the second time within a quarter of a century the nation, at first shocked and shamed, recovered and gained strength. Noble tributes abounded from around the world, but his lifetime friend, Richard Cardinal Cushing, pointed out in his eulogy that the President's own words were his most appropriate epitaph. And the dominant theme of those words was summed up by the new President: "Let us continue."

A EULOGY

A shocked and stricken world stands helpless before the fact of death, that death brought to us through a tragically successful assault upon the life of the President of the United States. Our earliest disbelief has slowly given way to unprecedented sorrow, as millions all over the earth join us in lamenting a silence that can never again be broken, and the absence of a smile that can never again be seen. For those of us who knew the President as friend as well as statesman, words mock our attempts to express the anguish of our hearts.

It was my privilege to have been associated with John F. Kennedy from the earliest days of his public life, to have watched him mature with ever-expanding responsibility, to have known some of the warmth of his hardy friendship, to see tested under pain and loss the steely strength of his character. I have been with him in joy and in sorrow, in decision and in crisis, among friends and with strangers, and I know of no one who has combined in more noble perfection the qualities of greatness that marked his calm, cool, calculating intelligence and his big, brave and bountiful heart. Now, all of a sudden, he has been taken from us and, I dare say, we shall not see his like again.

Many there are who will appropriately pay tribute to the President as a world figure, to his skill in political life, and to his devotion in public service. Many others will measure the wide interests of his mind, the swiftness of his resolution, the power of his persuasion, the efficiency of his action and the courage of his convictions.

For me, it is proper to recall him during these days of mourning, as husband and father, surrounded by his young and beloved family. Although the demands of his exalted position carried him often on long journeys and filled even his days at home with endless labors, how often he would make time to share with his little son and sweet daughter whatever time would be his own. What a precious treasure it is now, and will forever be, in the memories of two fatherless children! Who among us can forget those childish ways which, from time to time, enhanced the elegance of the executive mansion with the touching scenes of a happy family life! Charming Caroline "stealing" the publicity; jovial "John-John" on all fours ascending the stairs of an airplane to greet his "daddy," and the loving mother, like all mothers, joyfully watching the two children of her flesh and blood, mindful always of three others in the nurseries of Heaven.

At the side of the President, in understanding, devotion and affection, behold his gracious and beautiful Jacqueline! True always to the obligations of her role as mother, she has given new dimensions to the trying demands of being America's first lady. The pride in her husband, which he so eminently justified, was plainly

Richard Cardinal Cushing with the casket outside of St. Matthew's Cathedral.

reciprocated in his pride of her. The bond of love that made them one in marriage became like hoops of steel binding them together.

From wherever men may look out from eternity to see the workings of our world, John Kennedy must beam with new pride in that valiant woman who shared his life, especially to the moments of its early and bitter end. And, oh, that end; it will never be forgotten by her for her clothes were stained with the blood of her assassinated husband.

These days of sorrow must be more difficult for her than for any others but Divine Providence has blessed her, as few such women in history, by allowing her hero husband to have the dying comfort of her arms. When men speak of this sad hour in times to come, they will ever recall how well her frail beauty matched in courage the stalwart warrior who was her husband. We who had so many reasons for holding her person in a most profound respect, must now find an even wider claim for the nobility of her spirit.

One cannot think of the late President without thinking also of the legacy of public service which was bequeathed to him by his name and family. For several generations and in a variety of tasks, this republic, on one level or another, has been enriched by the blood that was so wantonly shed on Friday last. John Kennedy fulfilled in the highest office available to him, the long dedication of his family. It is a consolation for us all to know that his death does not spell the end of this public service but commits to new responsibilities the energies and abilities of one of the truly great families of America. What comfort can we extend to their heavy hearts today—mother, father, sisters, brothers—what beyond the knowledge that they have given to history a youthful Lincoln, who in his time and in his sacrifice, has made more sturdy the hopes of this nation and its people.

The late President was, even at death, a young man— and he was proud of that youth. Who can forget the words with which he began his short years as President:

"Let the word go forth from this time and place, to friend and foe alike, that the torch has been passed to a new generation of Americans—born in this century, tempered by war, disciplined by a hard and bitter peace, proud of our ancient heritage. . . ."

No words could describe better the man himself who spoke, one whose youth supplied an almost boundless energy, despite illness and physical handicaps, whose record in war touched heroic proportions, whose service in the Congress was positive and progressive. It was against this personal background that he continued by saying:

"Let every nation know . . . that we shall pay any price, bear any burden, meet any hardship, support any friend, oppose any foe to assure the survival and success of liberty.

"This much we pledge and more."

All that the young President promised in these words, he has delivered; he has written in unforgettable language his own epitaph. A few days ago, he was the leader of the free world, full of youth and promise; his was a role of action, full of conflict, excitement, pressure and change; his was a fully human life, one in which "he lived, felt dawn, saw sunset glow, loved and was loved." Now in the inscrutable ways of God, he has been summoned to an eternal life beyond all striving, where everywhere is peace.

All of us who loved this man—his youth, his drive, his ideals, his heart, his generosity, his hopes—mourn now more for ourselves and each other than for him. *We* will miss him; *he* only waits for us in another place. He speaks to us from there in the words of Paul to Timothy:

"As for me, my blood already flows in sacrifice.... I have fought the good fight; I have finished the race; I have redeemed the pledge: I look forward to the prize that awaits me, the prize I have earned. The Lord, Whose award never goes amiss, will grant it to me; to me, yes, and to all those who have learned to welcome His coming."

John F. Kennedy has fought the good fight for the God-given rights of his fellow man and for a world where peace and freedom shall prevail. He has finished the race at home and in foreign lands, alerting all men to the dangers and the hopes of the future, pledging aid in every form to those who were tempted to misinterpret his words, to become discouraged and to abandon themselves to false prophets. He has fulfilled unto death the pledge he made on the day of his inauguration—"I shall not shrink from my responsibilities."

Far more would he have accomplished for America and the world if it were not for his assassination here in his native land that he loved so much and for which he dedicated and gave his life.

May his noble soul rest in peace and may his memory be perpetuated in our hearts as a symbol of love for God, country and all mankind, the foundation upon which a new world must be built if our civilization is to survive.

RICHARD CARDINAL CUSHING
Boston, Massachusetts, Nov. 24, 1963

Mrs. Kennedy and daughter Caroline kneeling at casket in Capitol rotunda.

On the Presidential Coat of Arms, the American eagle holds in his right talon the olive branch, while in his left he holds a bundle of arrows. We intend to give equal attention to both.

State of the Union Address to Congress,
Washington, D.C., Jan. 30, 1961

A man may die, nations may rise and fall, but an idea lives on. Ideas have endurance without death.

Opening of the new USIA transmitter complex
at Greenville, North Carolina, Feb. 8, 1963

. . . This country is moving and it must not stop. It cannot stop. For this is a time for courage and a time of challenge. Neither conformity nor complacency will do. Neither the fanatics nor the fainthearted are needed. . . . So let us not be petty when our cause is so great. Let us not quarrel amongst ourselves when our nation's future is at stake. Let us stand together with renewed confidence in our cause—united in our heritage of the past and our hopes for the future—and determined that this land we love shall lead all mankind into new frontiers of peace and abundance.

To have been delivered at Austin, Texas, Nov. 22, 1963

. . . The final measure of your Administration will, in large measure, rest on how well you respond to [the American people's] inward hopes while leading them toward new horizons of ambition and achievement.

"John F. Kennedy Tells Youth How to Prepare for the Presidency,"
an article in Parade Magazine, Sept. 23, 1962

. . . On the Friday after next, I am to assume new and broader responsibilities. But I am not here to bid farewell to Massachusetts. For 43 years—whether I was in London, or in Washington, or in the South Pacific, or elsewhere—this has been my home. . . . The enduring qualities of Massachusetts—the common threads woven by the Pilgrim and the Puritan, the fisherman and the farmer, the Yankee and the immigrant—will not be and could not be forgotten in this nation's Executive Mansion. They are an indelible part of my life, my conviction, my view of the past and my hopes for the future.

Massachusetts Legislature, Boston, Massachusetts, Jan. 9, 1961

. . . I grew up in a very strict house, and one where there . . . were no free riders, and everyone was expected to . . . give their best to what they did. . . . There is no sense in trying to do anything unless you give it your maximum effort. You may not succeed, but at least the effort and dedication and interest should be there.

Television-Radio Program, "Presidential Countdown:
'Mr. Kennedy: A Profile,' " (CBS), Sept. 19, 1960

We meet in an hour of grief and challenge. Dag Hammarskjöld is dead. But the United Nations lives. His tragedy is deep in our hearts, but the task for which he died is at the top of our agenda. A noble servant of peace is gone. But the quest for peace lies before us.

UN General Assembly, New York, New York, Sept. 25, 1961

. . . There is a quotation from Lincoln which I think is particularly applicable today. He said, "I believe there is a God. I see the storm coming and I believe He has a hand in it. If He has a part and place for me, I believe that I am ready."

We see the storm coming, and we believe He has a hand in it, and if He has a place and a part for us, I believe that we are ready.

Presidential Prayer Breakfast, Washington, D.C., March 1, 1962

Photos by George P. Koshollek Jr.,
for the Milwaukee Journal

President Kennedy's family
leaving the Capitol.

Above: Funeral cortege with traditional riderless horse. Left: View of the Lincoln Memorial from Arlington National Cemetery as cortege crosses Potomac River. Below: Two women in White House grounds after President's death.

Above: Heads of state and other dignitaries from around the world at graveside.

Below: Changing of the guard at the grave after the funeral at Arlington National Cemetery.

THE UNDYING SPIRIT

We think of some Presidents, like James Monroe, primarily in terms of their acts; of others, like Grover Cleveland, primarily in terms of their traits. John F. Kennedy will live in history both for his deeds and his attributes—remarkably alike as a man of action and a man of character. In both aspects coming generations will study him.

Cruelly brief his Presidential career! But his masterful handling of the Cuban crisis in the autumn of 1962, terminating not only in the withdrawal of Soviet weapons and airmen but in a clarification of the whole Russo-American scene, will remain a landmark in the history of world affairs in our century. His part in the great international agreement to halt nuclear testing in the atmosphere was another memorable contribution to global safety. "Mankind must put an end to war—or war will put an end to mankind"—these words will haunt men's minds. He led in the boldest movement ever made for enlarging and enforcing civil rights in the United States; and although his successor will sign the measure for which he fought so hard, the chief credit will be his. His interest in the emergent new nations of Asia and Africa, and in helping to solve the ever-greater problems of Latin America, will not be forgotten in these three continents. The Alliance for Progress which absorbed so much of his energies and hopes may succeed or may fail. But this inspired effort to combat poverty by a program of wise economic activity, to substitute literacy for ignorance and to shame selfish groups into a support of social reform and civic decency can never fail so completely that it will not remain an object lesson for the future, undying in its influence.

And what of his traits? The quality of moral courage especially appealed to him in his study of historical figures, and he strove to show a valorous integrity in his own acts. After he died his *Profiles in Courage* rose to the head of the best-seller lists, for the nation wished to restudy his prime examples of spiritual intrepidity. But neither morally nor intellectually did he ever set himself apart from the people,

for his warmth of heart and gallantry of spirit never deserted him. Not subtlety, but rather a spacious simplicity marked his character; at times he seemed happily boyish. "He is always cheerful, never worries, and works incessantly"—this could be said of him as it was of Churchill. His ebullience and self-confidence helped give the country hope and firmness. It was part of his youthfulness of heart that he thought little of yesterday, much of today, but most of all of tomorrow. He realized that his Presidency fell in a revolutionary time, and was impatient with those who failed to see how fast economic and social change was overtaking the world overseas, and the people at home. The two grim questions always present in his mind were, "What will happen next?" and "How fast can we get ready for it?"

Hence he seemed impatient—as indeed he was. We and the world were tolerating too many hoary wrongs; we were drifting when we should be planning and acting. "Liberalism is not a creed but a frame of mind," he said. Like Franklin D. Roosevelt, he had a sympathetic and imaginative mind, so that in facing the needs of 1970 he could put himself into the shoes of a farmer, a mill hand, a clerk or an engineer. Like Teddy Roosevelt, he believed in swift and strenuous action—by plan. And yet he could be patient. Told that the record of the current Congress in its first year was abominably poor, he replied: "We must judge it by the whole two years of its life."

Always it was peace that was nearest his heart. At times he seemed warlike, for he dealt with threats of war, and he realized that peace must be armed with a sharp sword. He would have been pleased to think that he did something for justice and welfare in the United States, and in the struggling nations which America has sometimes all too grudgingly aided. But it would have pleased him most of all to think that history would record that his greatest achievements were his contributions to the peace and security of mankind; and this history will assuredly do.

ALLAN NEVINS

Overleaf: One of the honor guards in the East Room of the White House while the body of President Kennedy lay in state.